In the Chips

In the Chips

The Complete Chocolate Chip Cookbook

Peggy Mellody
and
Linda Rosenbloom

RAWSON ASSOCIATES: New York

Library of Congress Cataloging in Publication Data
Mellody, Peggy.
  In the chips.
  Includes index.
    1. Cookery (Chocolate)   I. Rosenbloom, Linda.
  II. Title.
  TX767.C5M45   1985   641.6'374   84-61933
  ISBN 0-89256-288-9

Published simultaneously in Canada by Collier Macmillan Canada, Inc.
Composition by P&M Typesetting, Inc., Waterbury, Connecticut
Manufactured by Fairfield Graphics, Fairfield, Pennsylvania
Designed by Jacques Chazaud
First Edition

TO OUR PARENTS

When the chips are down,
We can always count on you.

Contents

Acknowledgments

The most difficult part about writing a cookbook is keeping the author's weight down. Fortunately I have many friends (old and new) who unselfishly decided not to count calories while taste testing my chocolate experiments. Special thanks go to the SVAMC Marrow Transplant Unit staff, Janet Leahy, my housemates, my students, and my family (Pat, Vicki, Judy, Sean, Joe, and Tim). I deeply appreciate their support and encouragement throughout this entire project.

P. M.

Writing and researching a cookbook can be quite a task, but the real heroes in this case are those who kindly sampled the results of recipe testing and experimentation. Special thanks to those at Boeing and ONB (they know who they are) for lending their services as tasters. To the workers at the GMF in Tacoma, Washington, who were an indispensable source of taste testers and evaluations, a heartfelt thanks. Last, but not least, to Ron, Rick, and Ann, a sincere appreciation for their help with dispensing the goodies, their encouragement, and their confidence in the book. Thank you all.

L. R.

In the Chips

Before
You Begin This Book

Chocoholics who yearn for new ways to indulge their passion will find this book—the first complete chocolate chip cookbook—taking them down new pathways in culinary adventure. In nearly 300 innovative recipes and variations we show you how to use chips in every conceivable kind of sweet treat.

We are confirmed chocoholics, as are many of our friends and members of our families. We even run a food business largely focused on chocolate, called, aptly enough, In the Chips, since one of our specialties is giant chocolate chip cookies.

With more than thirty years of cooking experience between us, we began four years ago to search for unusual ways to use chocolate in cooking. We found what we were searching for when we began to work extensively with chocolate chips. We discovered chocolate chips are by far the most economical and versatile of all the baking chocolates. So we began experimenting with them in a wide variety of recipes. We came up with hundreds of ways to use chips and decided eventually that we would like to share our enthusiasm with other chocoholics, who, like so many, may not have realized the incredible array of creative cooking possibilities that chips offer beyond their use in cookies.

In this book you will find recipes and variations for breads, cakes, garnishes, candies, hot, cold, and frozen desserts, pies, ice creams, cookies, sauces, and beverages.

A gala holiday chapter explains how to make traditional Christmas treats more delicious by making them with chocolate chips.

In addition to recipes, the opening sections of our book offer invaluable advice about cooking with chocolate and chips in general and some really innovative counsel about buying, storing, and using general ingredients essential to chocolate cookery.

We show, first, why it is important to store chocolate not where most people think it should be—the refrigerator—but in an airtight container in a cool, dry place with a temperature range of between 60° to 75° F and a relative humidity of 50 percent or less. Then we show you how to store it for lengthy periods of time without damaging its fragile flavor, texture, or appearance.

Melting chocolate and chocolate chips is not just a matter of putting a pan on the fire; special techniques are required, and they are explained here step by step. Chocolate is heat-sensitive and scorches easily, so we explain how to avoid chocolate melting crises, how to add liquid or butter to melted chocolate, how to handle chocolate in a microwave— and more.

Next, you'll find something unique: a chocolate chip conversion table that shows you how to convert chocolate chips— which are difficult to measure—from ounces to cups, making measuring a snap.

Freshness, accurate measuring, and proper preparation of essential ingredients are vital to the successful outcome of a recipe. That's why we have included a definitive section showing how to buy, store, and handle properly such ingredients as butter, eggs, milk, whipping cream, flour, sugar, leavening, fruit, and nuts. Most cookbooks don't show you how to handle these ingredients to achieve the best results in a recipe. What you learn here will carry over to your cooking success in general.

We show you how to answer correctly every time that all-important question of what to substitute if you find at the last moment that you are out of an essential ingredient for a chocolate chip recipe. A clear chart shows you how to make do with substitute ingredients if you are out of flour, brown sugar, baking powder, an egg, whole milk, buttermilk, light cream, corn syrup, dry yeast, pumpkin pie spice, unsweetened chocolate.

Another feature is our chapter on garnishing with chocolate chips. Almost every sweet treat you can imagine can be embellished and made to look professional and sophisticated by using our easy garnishing techniques. We show you how to handle chocolate chips so that they behave and form into the shapes you want. There are layer garnishing techniques, chocolate curls, chocolate cutouts, chocolate noodles, chocolate walls, chocolate cones, chocolate rolls, liqueur fans, chocolate fruit dipping techniques, chocolate-covered coffee beans, chocolate-dipped almonds, chocolate leaves, chocolate cherries and strawberries, chocolate lacework and free-form garnishing—and we even show you how to write with chocolate.

The chapters that follow contain recipes for creating a variety of sweet treats and desserts employing chocolate chips. The bread chapter includes sweet breads, coffee cakes, muffins, rolls, and croissants. Thirty kinds of cake using chocolate chips give every creative cook nearly three variations of cake a month to work with. Twenty-six pies and variations based on chocolate chips will start creative cooking inspiration running for filling meal-end desserts. We have included twenty-nine kinds of candy you can make with chips and added a lot of varieties to stimulate your creativity.

Then there are hot, cold, and frozen desserts and ice creams, sauces, and beverages.

A special chapter offers recipes for celebrating Christmas with chocolate chip recipes of every kind.

And of course, there are recipes for cookies—nearly forty in all. But they go far beyond the ubiquitous chocolate chip cookie into such realms as Cinnamon Streusel Bars, Coffee Pecan Chip Bars, Sherry Walnut Treasure Bars, Coconut Chip Macaroons, Marshmallow Brownies, Melting Lace, Mocha Bonbons, and more.

We have had a wonderful time creating this book. We hope you, your family, and your friends have a wonderful time enjoying the treats that come out of it.

PART I

Handling
Chocolate
and Chips

The
Toll House Story

No sweeter revolution ever came out of the United States than the one that rocked the chocolate world, and it was all due to the miscalculations of the owner of a country inn in the 1930s.

In 1930, Kenneth and Ruth Wakefield purchased an old house in Whitman, Massachusetts that originally was a toll house, where horses were changed on the route between New Bedford and Boston. The Wakefields opened an inn and restaurant, calling it Toll House. One day Mrs. Wakefield was experimenting with the recipe of a colonial cookie called the butter drop-do. Having a bar of semisweet chocolate on hand, she chopped it into pieces and stirred the chunks of chocolate into the cookie dough.

Mrs. Wakefield assumed that the chocolate would melt and spread throughout each cookie, but she assumed wrongly. Instead, the chocolate bits held their shape and created a sensation. She called her creation Toll House Crunch Cookies. A visitor to the inn sampled Mrs. Wakefield's invention, then later described it to a friend who worked for a Boston newspaper.

Word of the cookie spread, and it became so popular that the Nestlé Company, seeing the potential, developed a scored semisweet chocolate bar with a small cutting implement so that making the chocolate chunks would be easier. Mrs. Wakefield's cookie recipe was printed on the wrapper of each bar. In 1939 Nestlé created convenient, ready-to-use chocolate pieces, introducing chocolate chips. In the 1940s Mrs. Wakefield sold all legal rights to the use of the Toll House trademark to Nestlé.

Today the chocolate chip cookie remains a favorite choice among cookie connoisseurs. The term *toll house* has become a part of the American language. So common in fact, that like thermos bottle and shredded wheat, *toll house* has become a generic term. On August 25, 1983, the Nestlé Company lost its exclusive rights to the trademark in federal court. *Toll house* is now a descriptive term for a cookie.

Storing
Chocolate and Chips

It is always a good idea to keep plenty of chocolate chips and other baking chocolate on hand in case there is a need to whip up something quick to satisfy a craving. Rules for storing the different types of chocolate are basically the same. They are as follows:

• Store chocolate in an airtight container.
• Chocolate should be kept in a cool, dry place. Storage temperature should range between 60° to 75°F, with a relative humidity of 50 percent or less.
• If longer storage is required, tightly wrap chocolate and freeze it. Chocolate may be frozen for from three to four months without changing its flavor, texture, or appearance.
• Improper storage of chocolate will cause it to develop a gray-white film or bloom. This discoloration is the result of some of the cocoa butter rising to the chocolate's surface. This bloom will not affect the quality or taste of the chocolate and will disappear as soon as the chocolate is melted.
• Unsweetened cocoa should be stored at the same temperature as other chocolates. It is less sensitive to temperature than other chocolates; however, if exposed to high temperatures or humidity, cocoa will lump together or lose some of its rich flavor and color.

Melting Chocolate

Some precautions should be taken when melting chocolate chips and other baking chocolates. The two basic rules for successfully melting chocolate are:

Rule I: The pan in which chocolate is being melted, and the utensil with which it is being stirred, must be absolutely dry. Any moisture less than 2 tablespoons per cup chocolate will cause the chocolate to become thick and unmanageable, to stiffen. Should this occur, add 1 to 2 teaspoons corn or peanut oil per ounce of chocolate, and stir until it becomes liquid again. (Do not use butter; it contains water.)

Rule II: Chocolate is heat-sensitive and scorches easily. For this reason, it should be melted over a low, gentle heat. If chocolate is being melted by itself, the double boiler is the best pot to use. Place the double boiler over simmering, not boiling, water, and stir until the chocolate is smooth. If chocolate is being melted with other ingredients, it is safe to melt it in a heavy saucepan over a direct low heat, stirring constantly to prevent scorching.

• If you add liquid or butter to melted chocolate, the amount added must be no less than 2 tablespoons per cup chocolate or the chocolate will stiffen.

• In order to melt chocolate chips safely over direct heat, they must be melted with at least ¼ cup liquid per cup chips.

• To melt a small amount of chocolate, place it in a cup, and set the cup into a pan of simmering water. Be very careful not to get any water into this mini double boiler.

• Chocolate may also be melted in a microwave oven. To do so, place chocolate in a microwave-proof dish, and melt it for 1 to 2 minutes. The chocolate will hold its shape, so upon its removal from the oven, stir it until smooth.

• To pick up every last bit of melted chocolate that clings to the pan, sprinkle over it a few teaspoons of the flour called for in the recipe. When the flour is stirred around the pan, the chocolate will be picked up, and there will be no waste.

Chocolate Chip Conversion Table

The following table is to help convert chocolate chips from ounces to cups.

2 ounces of chocolate chips = ⅓ cup

3 ounces of chocolate chips = ½ cup

4 ounces of chocolate chips = ⅔ cup

6 ounces of chocolate chips = 1 cup

8 ounces of chocolate chips = 1⅓ cups

9 ounces of chocolate chips = 1½ cups

10 ounces of chocolate chips = 1⅔ cups

12 ounces of chocolate chips = 2 cups

15 ounces of chocolate chips = 2½ cups

16 ounces of chocolate chips = 2⅔ cups

18 ounces of chocolate chips = 3 cups

What You Need to Know About Handling Other Essential Ingredients for Great Chocolate Chip Cooking

Freshness, accurate measuring, and proper preparation of essential ingredients are vital factors in the successful outcome of a recipe. First and foremost, carefully read a recipe *twice* before attempting to make it. This will help you make sure that the ingredients called for are on hand and prevent the gnashing of teeth and pulling of hair when you realize that the flour should have been sifted before being added (this is written from experience). On the following pages you will find some creative tips and preparation instructions for many of the main ingredients called for throughout this book, which will help you make your chocolate chip cookery a celebration for all.

BUTTER

Generally speaking, when a recipe calls for butter, margarine may be substituted; however, the end product will not be as rich and flavorful as it could be. If some butter flavor is desired, use half butter, half margarine in the recipe.

• There are two types of butters, salted and unsalted (sweet). All the recipes in this book were tested with salted butter. Use unsalted butter if specifically indicated in the ingredients list.

• Do not substitute for butter whipped butter, whipped margarine, or diet margarine when baking; they have more air and less fat than regular butter or margarine and will lead to an unsuccessful baked product.

• Vegetable shortening is not a reliable substitute for butter. If necessary, however, substitute vegetable shortening for *half* the butter called for in the recipe, except in the case of cream puffs.

• To soften frozen butter quickly, grate it through a coarse grater, and let it stand at room temperature for 15 minutes.

• Melt butter in a heavy saucepan over low heat.

• To brown butter, slowly heat it over a low heat until it is a light golden brown. Watch carefully so the butter will not burn and be useless.

• If a recipe calls for oil, most cooking oils available are above average grade, but for dietary reasons we recommend polyunsaturated vegetable oil.

EGGS

When using eggs, make sure that they are fresh and uncracked. Usually looking at an eggshell can determine whether or not it is fresh. The shell of an old egg is rather smooth and shiny, whereas a fresh eggshell is rough and chalky in appearance.

• To ensure even distribution, it is best to add eggs to a mixture one at a time, beating well after each addition.

• It is easier to separate eggs when they are cold.

• For greater volume, beat egg whites when they are at room temperature.

• Always use a clean, dry bowl when beating egg whites. Even a drop of water can hinder egg whites from being beaten properly.

• If a bit of egg yolk gets into the egg whites during separation, touch it with a damp paper towel to remove.

• Up to four egg whites can be beaten in a small mixing bowl; use a large mixing bowl for beating more.

• Do not beat egg whites in an aluminum bowl, or they may become discolored.

• For egg whites to retain their volume, they should be folded into the other ingredients immediately after being beaten.

MILK

There are three basic ways that whole milk is called for in the following recipes. Aside from calling for it to be poured directly from the carton, a recipe sometimes requires milk to be either soured or scalded. Here is how to prepare milk in these ways.

Sour Milk: Souring milk is relatively easy. Measure the souring agent into a measuring cup, and fill it to the desired amount with whole milk. The sour milk will be ready to use in 15 minutes. To make the amount of sour milk called for in a recipe, use the following proportions:

> ¾ teaspoon souring agent: ¼ cup sour milk
> 1 teaspoon souring agent: ⅓ cup sour milk
> 1½ teaspoons souring agent: ½ cup sour milk
> 1 tablespoon souring agent: 1 cup milk

• Either white vinegar or lemon juice may be used as the souring agent.
• For the best results, milk should be at room temperature before being soured.

Scalded Milk: To scald milk, pour the desired amount into a heavy saucepan. Place saucepan over medium-low heat, and warm milk until a ring of bubbles forms where the milk touches the pan.

• Before scalding milk, rinse saucepan with water to prevent scorching and sticking.
• Do not boil milk.

WHIPPING CREAM

Whipping cream is not difficult if the following tips are observed:
• Keep whipping cream in the refrigerator until ready to beat.
• Always use a clean bowl and beaters when whipping cream.
• Whipping cream will whip to a greater volume if the bowl and beaters are chilled before beating. Chill bowl and beaters in the refrigerator for at least 2 hours, or freeze them for 30 minutes.

• Beat whipping cream on medium-high speed. When it begins to thicken, watch it carefully. If whipping cream is overbeaten, it turns to butter.

FLOUR

There are three types of flour used in this book: bread flour, all-purpose flour, and cake flour. These flours vary in the amount of gluten present in them, bread flour having the highest gluten content, and cake flour having the least. Gluten affects such things as dough elasticity and texture. It is important to use the specific type of flour called for in a recipe's ingredient list. It is important to measure flour accurately. Too much or too little flour will alter the texture of the end product.

• Do not scoop flour into a measuring cup. Instead, spoon flour into measuring cup, and level it off with a spatula. Try not to tap or jar the cup while measuring flour.

• If a recipe calls for sifted flour, sift the flour before measuring.

SUGAR

Sugar is another ingredient that calls for close attention to be paid to its measuring.

• To measure granulated sugar, scoop it into a measuring cup and level it off with a spatula.

• To measure the correct amount of brown sugar, pack it firmly into a measuring cup, and level it off with a spatula.

• An easy way to sift confectioners' sugar is to press it through a fine-mesh strainer with a spoon.

• Granulated sugar may be substituted for confectioners' sugar if the latter is not available. Grind 1 cup granulated sugar and 1 tablespoon cornstarch in a blender until the mixture is powdery. (Be careful not to overgrind, or the sugar will caramelize.) This recipe will yield about 1½ cups confectioners' sugar.

LEAVENING

The success of a baked product depends on the freshness of the leavening used. To check for freshness, test leavening in the following manner:

Baking Powder: Stir ¼ teaspoon baking powder into 1 tablespoon water; if the mixture bubbles, it is fresh.

Baking Soda: Stir ¼ teaspoon baking soda into 1 tablespoon vinegar; if the mixture bubbles, it is fresh.

• Always be sure to mix baking powder and soda thoroughly with the other dry ingredients to ensure uniform leavening.

• A dough or batter that has to sit after baking powder has been activated (by adding water) will not fully expand. It is best to bake this type of mixture as soon as possible.

• Yeast that has been stored in the refrigerator should be brought to room temperature before being used.

• Dissolve active dry yeast in warm water (105° to 115°F) unless otherwise required. Compressed yeast should be dissolved in water no warmer than 95°F.

FRUIT

Next are a few tips to help prepare and preserve some of the fruits called for in the recipes that follow.

• Immediately toss sliced bananas in citrus or apple juice to prevent their browning. Also, a squirt of lemon juice in mashed bananas helps keep them white.

• When you use berries, it is best to wash them just before using. Washed and stored berries will not retain their firmness.

• To toast coconut, preheat oven to 350°F. Spread coconut on a jelly roll pan. Bake, stirring frequently, for 15 minutes.

• To help prevent dates from sticking to knife during chopping, lightly oil the blade.

• To plump raisins, simmer them in water or orange juice for 5 minutes.

NUTS

Nuts add a taste all their own to desserts and baked goods. Following are the ways of preparing them called for in this book:

Blanching Almonds: To blanch almonds, bring a saucepan of water to a full boil. Put almonds in the boiling water, and heat, stirring, for 1 minute. Drain almonds, and rinse them in cold water. Gently squeeze almonds out of their skins. (Be careful, they are very slippery.)

• Blanched almonds may be dried on a jelly roll pan in a 200°F oven for about 30 minutes if desired. (Do not brown.)

• To sliver almonds, let them sit in the boiling water until it cools to room temperature. Remove skins, and cut the almonds with a sharp knife. Dry, using directions above.

Skinning Hazelnuts: To skin hazelnuts, place them on a jelly roll pan, and bake in a 350°F oven for 15 minutes, or until their skins began to parch and flake off. Remove from oven. When they may be handled, rub hazelnuts between clean coarse kitchen towels until most of the skins are removed. Pick out the nuts, and discard the skins. (A few bits of skin may adhere to hazelnuts.) Another way to remove hazelnut skins is to place the warm nuts into a brown paper bag and rub them together to loosen skins.

Toasting Nuts: To toast nuts, preheat oven to 300°F. Place lightly oiled nuts on a jelly roll pan. Toast for 10 to 15 minutes, stirring occasionally for even browning.

• To oil nuts, toss them in a plastic bag; use 1 teaspoon oil per cup nuts.

Grinding Nuts: Two basic tools can be used for grinding nuts; the hand-held grinder and the food processor. A blender will not evenly grind nuts.

• If you are grinding nuts in a food processor, add a little sugar to prevent them from sticking and becoming oily.

Substitution Table

It is always best to use the specific ingredients called for in a recipe. But if you are in a bind, the following substitutions generally are acceptable.

If You Do Not Have:	*Use:*
1 cup cake flour	1 cup *less* 2 tablespoons all-purpose flour
½ cup brown sugar	½ cup granulated sugar mixed with 2 tablespoons molasses
1 whole egg	2 egg yolks
1 teaspoon baking powder	1 teaspoon baking soda *plus* 1 teaspoon cream of tartar
1 tablespoon cornstarch	2 tablespoons all-purpose flour
1 cup whole milk	½ cup evaporated milk *plus* ½ cup water
1 cup buttermilk	1 cup sour milk (see page 17)

If You Do Not Have:	*Use:*
1 cup light cream	2 tablespoons butter *plus* 1 cup milk *less* 2 tablespoons
1 cup corn syrup	1 cup water *plus* ¼ cup sugar
1 package active dry yeast	1 cake compressed yeast
½ cup raisins	½ cup prunes, chopped
2 teaspoons pumpkin pie spice	1 teaspoon cinnamon, ½ teaspoon ginger, and ¼ teaspoon each nutmeg and cloves
1 ounce unsweetened chocolate	3 tablespoons unsweetened cocoa blended with 1 tablespoon butter or vegetable shortening

Garnishing
with Chocolate Chips

Nothing dresses up a dessert more than garnishing, and chocolate chips lend themselves beautifully to the task. From simple curls to intricate lacework, chocolate chips have shown themselves to be extremely versatile. Following are a multitude of tips and recipes for using chocolate chips as garnishes and suggestions for the types of desserts they might enhance. Have no fear when garnishing with chocolate chips, for accidents and leftovers may be remelted and reused.

• Chocolate garnishes may be made in advance. To store, place them in a rigid airtight plastic container with a sheet of wax paper between layers of garnishes. Chill until ready to use. Do not freeze, or the garnishes will develop a white film on their surfaces.
• Try to handle garnishes as little as possible. When it is necessary to handle them, rinse your hands in cool water and dry them. This cools down hands and helps prevent them from melting the garnishes.
• Chocolate cones, curls, and rolls melt easily if handled. The best way to transfer them is with a toothpick. Chocolate cutouts and leaves can be moved from work surface to dessert with a spatula.
• Lift garnishes, such as Liqueur Fans, from wax paper with a small knife.

• An easy way to ice down a countertop is to set a $13 \times 9 \times 2$-inch pan filled with ice water on it; let it stand for 15 minutes, remove, and start working with chocolate garnishes. Move the pan around if a larger iced surface is desired.

CHOCOLATE LAYER GARNISHING TECHNIQUE

One of the simplest forms of garnishing with chocolate chips is to melt and spread them out to a thin layer on a flat surface. There are two methods of doing this. First, the melted chocolate chips may be spread out on a chilled marble slab or iced countertop. Let the chocolate stand at room temperature for about 2 hours, or until it is set and loses its gloss. The second, quicker method is to spread out melted chocolate chips on a cookie sheet, and refrigerate until set. After the chocolate is set, let it stand at room temperature for a few minutes to soften it slightly. The following recipes are ways the chocolate layer technique may be applied to garnishing.

Chocolate Curls

One of the most common types of garnish, Chocolate Curls are suitable for all sorts of desserts.

½ cup semisweet chocolate chips

Melt chocolate chips in top of a double boiler over simmering water, stirring until smooth. Using desired method (see above), spread melted chocolate chips out to a 1¼-inch-thick layer. Allow chocolate to set. To make curls, pull a sharp straight-edged knife held at an angle across chocolate layer. The more horizontally the knife is held, the larger the curls will be. Remember, when you make Chocolate Curls, practice makes perfect. Transfer curls to dessert, or chill until ready to use.

Chocolate Cutouts I

Chocolate Cutouts are a very versatile and pretty way to garnish.

½ cup semisweet chocolate chips

Melt chocolate chips in top of a double boiler over simmering water, stirring until smooth. Place a sheet of wax paper over work surface. Using desired method (page 24), spread melted chocolate chips out to an ⅛-inch-thick layer. Allow chocolate to set. Cut chocolate into desired shapes with small cookie cutters or a sharp small knife. Separate Chocolate Cutouts from wax paper. Transfer cutouts to dessert, or chill until ready to use.

FLEXIBLE CHOCOLATE GARNISHING TECHNIQUE

Flexible Chocolate is another way to use chocolate chips for garnishing. With the addition of butter and corn syrup, the chocolate becomes pliable, yet it will hold its shape when chilled. The following is the basic recipe for Flexible Chocolate.

Flexible Chocolate

Makes about ¾ cup

1 cup semisweet chocolate chips
1 tablespoon butter
1 tablespoon light corn syrup

Melt chocolate chips and butter with corn syrup in top of a double boiler over simmering water, stirring until smooth. Remove from heat; leave double boiler over water. Use Flexible Chocolate as directed below.

Chocolate Cutouts II: Another way to prepare Chocolate Cutouts uses Flexible Chocolate.

Tear four 15-inch-long sheets of wax paper. Place one piece each on two cookie sheets. Spoon half the melted Flexible Chocolate onto the wax paper on one of the prepared cookie sheets; top with a second piece of wax paper, roll chocolate out ⅛ inch thick with a rolling pin. Repeat procedure on the other cookie sheet. Chill chocolate until set. Peel off the top sheet of wax paper, and let chocolate stand at room temperature for about 5 minutes. Cut chocolate into desired shapes with a sharp knife or small cookie cutter. Lift cutouts off wax paper with a spatula. Transfer Chocolate Cutouts to dessert, or chill until ready to use.

Note: If Chocolate Cutouts are too soft to remove from wax paper, chill them for a few minutes until firm; then try again.

Chocolate Noodles: Chocolate Noodles are great for garnishing cakes, ice cream, mousses, etc.

Tear four 15-inch-long sheets of wax paper. Place one piece each on two cookie sheets. Spoon half the Flexible Chocolate onto the wax paper on one of the prepared cookie sheets; top with a second piece of wax paper; roll chocolate out ⅛ inch thick with a rolling pin. Repeat procedure on the other cookie sheet. Chill chocolate until set. Peel off top sheet of wax paper, and let chocolate stand at room temperature for about 5 minutes, until slightly soft. Cut chocolate into ¼-inch-wide strips with a sharp knife (be careful not to cut the wax paper). Peel Chocolate Noodles off wax paper, and drape on dessert.

Chocolate Wall: Dress up a cake or torte by encircling it with a Chocolate Wall.

Tear two sheets of wax paper 3 inches longer than the circumference of the cake or torte being garnished; place one piece on a cookie sheet (if the wax paper is too long, cut it in half). Spoon Flexible Chocolate into a line down the center of the wax paper. Place the second sheet of paper over chocolate; roll out to an ⅛-inch-thick and 2-inch-wide strip with a rolling pin. (For a taller cake and thus a wider strip, a double recipe of Flexible Chocolate may be needed.) Chill until chocolate is set. Peel off the top sheet of wax paper. Cut through chocolate and wax paper with a sharp knife to make a strip as wide as the side of the cake or torte. Wrap strip, paper side out, around cake or torte, overlapping the ends. Peel wax paper back 1½ inches at each end, and press together. Smooth over the seam with a knife, dipped into hot water and dried. (Longer walls should be slightly overlapped and joined in the same manner.) Peel off remaining wax paper. Chill until ready to serve.

TECHNIQUE FOR SPREADING CHOCOLATE ONTO FORMS

Spreading melted chocolate chips onto wax paper forms is yet another way to make garnishes. The following various types of garnishes use this method.

Chocolate Cones

Makes 1 dozen

Set atop cakes, mousses, soufflés, or tortes, Chocolate Cones will lend an elegant look.

⅓ cup semisweet chocolate chips

Cut twelve 5-inch circles out of wax paper; fold circles in half. To shape a cone, take a half circle, and twist the straight edges around, overlapping them, until they line up. Secure the outside edge with a small piece of tape. (Make sure that the tip of the cone is tightly closed, or the chocolate will drip through.) Repeat procedure with all the wax paper half circles.

Melt chocolate chips in top of a double boiler over simmering water, stirring until smooth. Remove from heat; keep double boiler over water. Spread a teaspoonful of melted chocolate chips in each cone with a small paintbrush or pointed knife to coat completely. Place cones on a plate. Refrigerate until chocolate is set. When chocolate is set, gently peel off wax paper. Garnish dessert with cones, or chill until ready to use.

Note: For a special touch, fill Chocolate Cones with sweetened whipped cream.

Chocolate Rolls

Makes 1 dozen

Chocolate Rolls may be used to garnish just about any type of dessert.

¼ cup semisweet chocolate chips

Cut twelve 3-inch circles out of wax paper; place on a cookie sheet. Melt chocolate chips in top of a double boiler over simmering water, stirring until smooth. Remove from heat; keep double boiler over water. Spread 1 teaspoon of melted chocolate chips onto each circle. Cool to room temperature. Then place circles in the refrigerator, and let harden. When cirlces are hard, remove from refrigerator, and let stand at room temperature for a few minutes. As chocolate softens and becomes pliable, roll by slowly folding wax paper over itself. Peel off wax paper from chocolate as it is rolled. Garnish dessert with Chocolate Rolls, or chill until ready to use.

Liqueur Fans

Makes 16

A hint of a favorite liqueur will add flavor to Liqueur Fans.

½ cup semisweet chocolate chips
2 tablespoons liqueur

Cover a cookie sheet with a piece of wax paper, and draw two 6-inch circles on the paper; set aside. Melt chocolate chips in top of a double boiler over simmering water, stirring until smooth. Remove from heat; stir in liqueur. Evenly spread melted chocolate mixture on the prepared circles about 1¼ inch thick. Place circles in the refrigerator, and let stand at room temperature for 5 minutes. Cut circles into eight equal wedges with a sharp small knife.

Note: Liqueur Triangles can also be made by spreading melted chocolate chips onto 5-inch squares; cut when cooled to form triangles.

DIPPED GARNISHING TECHNIQUES

Coffee beans, nuts, leaves, and fruits dipped in melted chocolate chips make unusual and interesting garnishes for desserts.

Chocolate-Covered Coffee Beans

Chocolate-Covered Coffee Beans can either garnish a variety of desserts or be eaten as is.

⅓ cup semisweet chocolate chips
¼ cup roasted coffee beans

Cover a cookie sheet with wax paper; set aside. Melt chocolate chips in top of a double boiler over simmering water, stirring until smooth. Remove from heat; keep double boiler over water. Using a fork, dip roasted coffee beans into melted chocolate chips, coating well; allow excess chocolate to drip back into pan. Place coated beans on prepared cookie sheet. Allow chocolate to set. Garnish dessert with Chocolate-Covered Coffee Beans, or chill until ready to use.

Chocolate-Dipped Almonds

Chocolate-Dipped Almonds are a cut above plain almond garnishes.

> *¼ cup semisweet chocolate chips*
> *½ cup blanched whole almonds*

Cover a cookie sheet with wax paper; set aside. Melt chocolate chips in top of a double boiler over simmering water, stirring until smooth. Remove from heat; keep double boiler over water. Dip each almond half way into melted chocolate chips; allow excess chocolate to drip back into pan. Place dipped almonds on prepared cookie sheet. Chill until chocolate is set.

Note: Do not limit this recipe to almonds. Hazelnuts, pecans, and walnuts are good, too.

Chocolate Leaves

Chocolate Leaves make a nice garnish, but be careful not to use poisonous leaves or leaves that have been sprayed with a pesticide when making them. Rose, orange, geranium, and mint leaves are safe.

Leaves (see recommendations, above)
¼ cup semisweet chocolate chips

Cover a cookie sheet with wax paper; set aside. Wash and gently pat dry leaves. Melt chocolate chips in top of a double boiler over simmering water, stirring until smooth. Remove from heat; keep double boiler over water. Pull bottom of each leaf over surface of melted chocolate chips to coat; remove excess chocolate by tapping leaf against side of pan. (Be sure that no chocolate gets onto top side of the leaf.) Place leaves, chocolate sides up, on prepared cookie sheet. Chill until chocolate is set. If chocolate has dripped onto the other side of any of the leaves, scrape clean with a sharp small knife, and return them to the refrigerator for a few minutes. Carefully peel each leaf from chocolate (this is not necessary with mint leaves). Garnish dessert, or chill Chocolate Leaves until ready to use.

Cordial Cherries

Makes 1 dozen

Cordial Cherries will dress up anything from cakes to ice cream.

12 maraschino cherries with stems
¼ cup brandy
⅔ cup semisweet chocolate chips

Combine maraschino cherries and brandy in a small bowl; place in freezer for 1 hour.

Place a sheet of wax paper on a plate. Melt chocolate chips in top of a double boiler over simmering water, stirring until smooth. Keep chocolate warm. Remove frozen cherries from brandy; pat dry. Dip cherries into melted chocolate chips, swirling to coat. Place completed cherries on prepared plate. Chill Cordial Cherries until ready to use.

Chocolate-Covered Strawberries

Makes 18 to 20 strawberries

For a delightful treat, garnish a dessert with fresh strawberries dipped in chocolate, or enjoy them alone.

1 pint strawberries with hulls intact
⅔ cup semisweet chocolate chips
4 tablespoons butter

Cover a cookie sheet with wax paper; set aside. Wash and pat dry strawberries. Melt chocolate chips and butter in top of a double boiler over simmering water, stirring until smooth. Remove from heat; keep double boiler over water. Dip each strawberry, two-thirds the way up, into melted chocolate mixture; allow excess chocolate to drip off. Place completed strawberries on prepared cookie sheet. Allow chocolate to set. Garnish dessert with Chocolate-Covered Strawberries, or chill until ready to use.

WRITING WITH CHOCOLATE

Chocolate chips are quite fluid when melted. They are an excellent substance to use for writing on cakes and other baked goods.

Chocolate Writing

There is no sweeter way to say "Happy Birthday"!

¼ to ½ cup semisweet chocolate chips

Melt chocolate chips in top of a double boiler over simmering water, stirring until smooth. Remove from heat; let cool for a few minutes. Spoon melted chocolate chips into a pastry bag with an ⅛-inch round tip. Chocolate in this form is very brittle when dry, so it is best to write immediately, directly onto whatever is being decorated.

Chocolate Lacework

Flexible Chocolate is a good substance not only for writing but also for making lacy designs on desserts. Let your imagination go, and come up with some interesting garnishing.

Ingredients for Flexible Chocolate, page 25

Prepare Flexible Chocolate as directed. Spoon melted chocolate into a pastry bag with an ⅛- or ¼-inch round tip. Design may be piped either directly onto dessert or onto a cookie sheet covered with wax paper. If piping design onto a prepared cookie sheet, carefully peel away wax paper and place decoration on dessert.

FREE-FORM CHOCOLATE CHIP GARNISHING

Last, but not least, chocolate chips in their natural state can be used for garnishing. Whether they are scattered over ice cream or used to make a geometric design on the top of a cheesecake, they are a welcome addition to any dessert.

A valuable tool for garnishing may be found in practically every kitchen: the potato peeler. For a quick and simple garnish, spread ⅓ cup melted chocolate chips out to a ¼-inch-thick layer. Allow chocolate to set. When it is set, turn it on its side, and using a potato peeler, shave off small curls of chocolate. Transfer chocolate shavings to dessert.

PART II

Recipes

Chocolate Chip Breads

The chapter that follows opens up a whole new world to chocoholics. It permits you to indulge in chocolate chips in the morning as well as at noon and night. Aficionados can start the day with breakfasts that include chip-filled muffins, coffee cakes, yeast rolls, and more—a sure way to make getting up a pleasure instead of a penalty. There are different kinds of breads, muffins, and coffee cakes in the pages that follow. Try them at meals; try them as snacks (what makes a more pleasing bedtime snack than a warm slice of chip and nut sweet bread?). Your family and friends will cheer. The chips add a truly distinctive and luscious taste to your baked treats.

Cherry-Chip Nut Bread *39*
Chocolate Nut Bread *40*
Lemon Chip Bread *40*
Orange and Chip Nut Bread *41*
Rummy Walnut Chip Loaf *42*
Chocolate-Pecan-Topped Coffee Cake *43*
Jam Swirl Coffee Cake *44*
Almond Chocolate Braid *45*
Chocolate Chip Ring *46*
Marmalade Lattice Coffee Cake *48*
Mocha Chip Coffee Cake *49*
Banana Chip Muffins *50*
Chocolate Chip Oatmeal Muffins *51*
Peanut Butter Chip Muffins *51*
Streusel Pecan Chip Muffins *52*
Babas au Rhum *53*
PB & J Rolls *54*
Glazed Cheesecake Chip Rolls *56*
Orange Chip Rolls *57*
Chocolate-Filled Croissants *58*

Cherry-Chip Nut Bread

1 loaf

2¼ cups all-purpose flour   3 tablespoons oil
¾ cup granulated sugar   ½ teaspoon almond extract
3 teaspoons baking powder   ½ cup candied cherries,
1 egg, beaten   chopped
¾ cup milk   ½ cup nuts, chopped
                                   ½ cup mini chocolate chips

ALMOND GLAZE
⅔ cup confectioners' sugar,   ¼ teaspoon almond extract
   sifted   ¼ cup mini chocolate chips
2 teaspoons milk

Grease and flour a 9 × 5 × 3-inch loaf pan; set aside. Preheat oven to 350°F. Stir together flour, granulated sugar, and baking powder in a large bowl. Blend beaten egg, milk, oil, and almond extract in a small bowl. Mix liquid ingredients into dry ingredients, stirring until just moistened. Fold in candied cherries, chopped nuts, and mini chocolate chips. Pour batter into prepared pan. Bake for 50 to 55 minutes, or until cake tester inserted in center comes out clean. Cool for 10 minutes in pan; then turn bread out onto wire rack. Cool completely.

For almond glaze, beat together sifted confectioners' sugar, milk, and almond extract in a small bowl, until smooth. Spread glaze over cooled bread; sprinkle with mini chocolate chips.

Store overnight.

Chocolate Nut Bread

1 loaf

⅓ cup semisweet chocolate   1 cup milk
    chips   ¼ cup oil
1¾ cups all-purpose flour   1 teaspoon vanilla
½ cup granulated sugar   1 cup nuts, chopped
1¼ teaspoons baking powder   ¼ cup nuts, chopped
1 egg, beaten   ¼ cup mini chocolate chips

   Grease a 9 × 5 × 3-inch loaf pan; flour bottom. Preheat oven to
350°F. Melt chocolate chips in a measuring cup set in a pan of simmering water, stirring until smooth. Remove from heat. Stir together
flour, sugar, and baking powder in a large bowl. Blend beaten egg,
milk, oil, and vanilla in a small bowl. Mix liquid ingredients into
dry ingredients, stirring until just moistened. Fold in melted chocolate and 1 cup chopped nuts. Pour batter into prepared pan; sprinkle with ¼ cup chopped nuts and mini chocolate chips. Bake for 50
to 65 minutes, or until cake tester inserted in center comes out
clean. Cool in pan for 15 minutes; then turn bread out onto wire
rack. Cool completely.

Bake quick breads in the lower third of oven; this prevents the top
of the loaf from overbrowning.

Lemon Chip Bread

1 loaf

2 cups all-purpose flour   2 eggs, beaten
2½ teaspoons baking powder   ½ cup milk

¾ *cup granulated sugar*   ½ *teaspoon vanilla*
2 *teaspoons grated lemon peel*   ½ *cup semisweet chocolate*
¼ *cup butter, softened*   *chips, chopped*

Grease a 9 × 5 × 3-inch loaf pan; flour bottom. Preheat oven to 350°F. Stir together flour, baking powder, sugar, and lemon peel in a large bowl. Cut in butter with a pastry blender or two knives used scissor-fashion until mixture resembles fine crumbs. Stir in beaten eggs, milk, and vanilla until just moistened (batter may be lumpy). Fold in chopped chocolate chips. Pour batter into prepared pan. Bake for 50 to 60 minutes, or until cake tester inserted comes out clean. Cool in pan for 10 minutes, then turn bread out onto wire rack. Cool completely.

Orange and Chip Nut Bread

1 loaf

2¼ *cups all-purpose flour,*   1 *tablespoon grated orange peel*
   sifted   1 *egg, beaten*
¾ *cup granulated sugar*   ¾ *cup orange juice*
2¼ *teaspoons baking powder*   ¼ *cup oil*
¼ *teaspoon baking soda*   ¾ *cup mini chocolate chips*
¾ *cup nuts, chopped*

   ORANGE GLAZE
½ *cup confectioner's sugar,*   2 *to 3 teaspoons orange liqueur*
   sifted   *or juice*
½ *teaspoon grated orange peel*

Grease a 9 × 5 × 3-inch loaf pan; flour bottom. Preheat oven to 350°F. Stir together sifted flour, granulated sugar, baking powder, and baking soda in a large bowl. Add chopped nuts and orange peel. Blend together beaten egg, orange juice, and oil in a small bowl. Mix liquid ingredients into dry ingredients, stirring until just moistened. Fold in mini chocolate chips. Pour batter into prepared pan. Bake for 55 to 60 minutes, or until cake tester inserted in center comes out clean. Cool in pan for 15 minutes; then turn bread out onto wire rack. Cool completely.

Wrap and store overnight.

For orange glaze, beat together sifted confectioners' sugar, orange peel, and orange liqueur in a small bowl until smooth. Spread glaze over bread; allow to set.

Variation: For Orange and Chip Nut Muffins, line sixteen muffin tins. Preheat oven to 400°F. Prepare batter as above, fill muffin tins two-thirds full. Bake for 15 to 20 minutes. Cool in tins for 15 minutes; then turn muffins out onto wire rack. Glaze muffins if desired.

Nut breads should be stored for at least 1 day before serving. This allows the flavors to blend, and the loaf will be easier to slice. Also, most quick breads freeze well for up to 3 months. To freeze, completely cool loaf; wrap first in plastic wrap and then in aluminum foil. Defrost bread at room temperature.

Rummy Walnut Chip Loaf

1 loaf

1½ cups walnuts, chopped coarse	2 teaspoons baking powder
½ cup semisweet chocolate chips	¼ cup butter, softened
2 tablespoons all-purpose flour	2 eggs, beaten
1¾ cups all-purpose flour	¼ cup milk
¾ cup brown sugar, packed firm	¼ cup dark rum
	1 teaspoon vanilla

Grease a 9 × 5 × 3-inch loaf pan; flour bottom. Preheat oven to 350°F. Toss together chopped walnuts and chocolate chips with 2 tablespoons flour in a bowl, set aside. Stir together 1¾ cups flour, brown sugar, and baking powder in a large bowl. Cut in butter with a pastry blender or two knives used scissor-fashion until mixture resembles fine crumbs. Combine beaten eggs, milk, rum, and vanilla in a small bowl. Mix liquid ingredients into dry ingredients, stirring until just moistened. Fold in chopped nut mixture. Pour batter into prepared pan. Bake for 1 hour and 20 minutes, or until cake tester inserted in center comes out clean. Cool in pan for 10 minutes; then turn bread out onto wire rack. Cool completely.

Note: Rummy Walnut Chip Loaf may be frozen for up to 1 month. To thaw, let bread stand at room temperature for 2 hours before serving.

Variation: For Amaretto Chip Loaf, substitute chopped almonds for walnuts and amaretto liqueur for rum. Bake as directed.

When mixing liquid ingredients into dry, stir just to moisten. Overmixing will activate the gluten in the flour, causing the bread to be tough.

Chocolate-Pecan-Topped Coffee Cake

12 servings

CHOCOLATE-PECAN TOPPING

¾ cup brown sugar, packed firm

1 tablespoon all-purpose flour

2 tablespoons butter, softened

1 cup pecans, chopped

½ cup mini chocolate chips

BATTER

2 cups all-purpose flour, sifted

1 teaspoon baking powder

1 teaspoon baking soda

½ cup butter, softened

1 cup granulated sugar

3 eggs, at room temperature

1 cup sour cream

½ cup golden raisins

For chocolate-pecan topping, stir together brown sugar and flour in a bowl. Cut in butter with a pastry blender or two knives used scissor-fashion until mixture resembles coarse crumbs. Stir in chopped pecans and mini chocolate chips; set aside.

Grease a 13 × 9 × 2-inch pan. Preheat oven to 350°F. For batter, stir together sifted flour, baking powder, and baking soda in a bowl. Cream together butter and sugar in a large mixing bowl on medium speed until light and fluffy. Add eggs, one at a time, blending well after each addition. Lower speed, and alternately add flour mixture with sour cream; blend well. Stir in raisins with a spoon. Spread batter into prepared pan; sprinkle with chocolate-pecan topping. Bake for 30 minutes, or until cake tester inserted in center comes out clean. Serve either warm or cool.

Variation: For Pecan-Chip Ribbon Coffee Cake, pour one-third batter into a greased and floured 10-inch tube pan. Sprinkle with half of filling mixture. Gently pour second third of batter over filling in pan, and top with remaining filling; pour remaining third of batter over filling. Bake for 55 to 60 minutes, or until cake tester inserted in center comes out clean. Scatter ½ cup semisweet chocolate chips on top of coffee cake, and return to oven for 1 minute. Remove from oven, and swirl chocolate chips over cake, allowing some of the cake to show through. Cool for 15 minutes in pan; then turn coffee cake out onto a serving plate. Cool.

When making quick and yeast breads, bring refrigerated ingredients, such as eggs and milk, to room temperature before using.

Jam Swirl Coffee Cake

---

9 servings

¾ cup all-purpose flour
⅔ cup granulated sugar
⅔ cup butter, softened
2 teaspoons baking powder
½ teaspoon baking soda
2 eggs

1¼ cups all-purpose flour
⅔ cup buttermilk or sour milk
⅓ cup jam
⅓ cup semisweet chocolate
    chips

Grease a 9-inch square pan; set aside. Preheat oven to 375°F. Stir together ¾ cup flour and sugar in a small mixing bowl. Cut in butter with a pastry blender or two knives used scissor-fashion, until mixture resembles coarse crumbs. Reserve ½ cup crumb mixture for topping. To remaining crumb mixture add baking powder, baking soda, and eggs one at a time, beating well after each addition. Beat on medium speed until light and fluffy. Lower speed, and alternately add 1¼ cups flour with buttermilk, blending well. Pour batter into prepared pan. Spoon jam over batter, and swirl with a knife to marbleize; sprinkle with chocolate chips. Crumble reserved crumb mixture over top. Bake for 40 minutes, or until cake tester inserted in center comes out clean. Cool; serve from pan.

Almond Chocolate Braid

---

1 coffee cake

DOUGH

1 package active dry yeast
½ cup lukewarm water (110°
  to 115°F)
2 egg yolks, at room
  temperature
¼ cup granulated sugar
¼ teaspoon salt

¼ teaspoon cardamom
½ cup all-purpose flour
2 tablespoons butter
1½ cups all-purpose flour
6 tablespoons butter, softened

ALMOND CHOCOLATE FILLING

¼ cup semisweet chocolate
  chips
2 egg whites
1 cup ground almonds

1 cup confectioners' sugar,
  sifted
½ teaspoon almond extract

TOPPING

2 teaspoons beaten egg white
2 tablespoons sliced almonds

2 teaspoons granulated sugar

For dough, lightly grease a large bowl; set aside. Dissolve yeast in lukewarm water in another large bowl. Lightly beat egg yolks in a small bowl. Stir beaten egg yolks, granulated sugar, salt, carda-mom, and ½ cup flour into yeast mixture. Melt 2 tablespoons but-ter; stir into batter with 1½ cups flour to make a moderately soft dough. Knead dough on a lightly floured surface until smooth. Place dough in prepared bowl; turn once. Cover bowl, and put in a warm, draft-free place. Allow dough to double, about 1 to 1½ hours.

When dough has doubled, return to floured surface, and roll out into a 14 × 10-inch rectangle; spread with 4 tablespoons butter. Fold dough into thirds crosswise, making three layers. Give dough a quarter turn. Once again roll out into a 14 × 10-inch rectangle. Spread with remaining 2 tablespoons butter, and fold again into thirds. Let dough rest while preparing filling.

For almond chocolate filling, melt chocolate chips in top of dou-ble boiler over simmering water, stirring until smooth. Remove from heat. Beat egg whites in a small mixing bowl on high speed until foamy; reserve 2 teaspoons for brushing over braid. Stir in ground almonds, melted chocolate, sifted confectioners' sugar, and almond extract with a spoon; set aside.

Grease a 9-inch springform or tube pan. To assemble braid, roll dough into a 13 × 9-inch rectangle. Cut lengthwise into three equal strips. Spoon filling down center of each strip. Close edges over fill-ing, pinching to seal. Braid strips together. Place, seam down, into prepared pan, forming a ring. Let braid rise until double, about 45 minutes to 1 hour.

Preheat oven to 350°F. For topping, brush braid with reserved egg white; sprinkle with sliced almonds and sugar. Bake for 35 to 45 minutes, or until well browned. Cool in pan for 10 minutes; then turn coffee cake out onto serving plate. Serve warm or cold.

Chocolate Chip Ring

6 servings

COFFEE CAKE

1 cup all-purpose flour	1½ teaspoons vanilla
1 package active dry yeast	¾ cup all-purpose flour

¼ *cup butter*
½ *cup milk*
¼ *cup granulated sugar*
1 *egg, at room temperature*

½ *cup nuts, chopped*
½ *cup semisweet chocolate*
  chips

GLAZE
½ *cup confectioners' sugar,*
  sifted

½ *teaspoon vanilla*
1 *to 2 teaspoons milk*

Generously grease a 4½-cup ring mold; set aside. For coffee cake, stir together 1 cup flour and yeast in a large mixing bowl. Melt butter with milk and granulated sugar in a heavy saucepan over low heat; stirring constantly, until warm (105° to 115°F). Add warmed mixture to dry ingredients. Add egg and vanilla; blend well. Beat mixture on low speed for 1 minute. Increase speed to high, and beat for 3 minutes. Stir in ¾ cup flour with a spoon. Stir in chopped nuts and chocolate chips, mixing well. Turn dough into prepared pan. Cover and let rise in a warm, draft-free place until dough is double, about 1 hour.

Preheat oven to 400°F. Bake for 12 to 15 minutes or until golden brown.

Meanwhile, for glaze, beat together sifted confectioners' sugar, vanilla, and milk in a small bowl until smooth. Immediately upon removing from oven, remove coffee cake from pan; drizzle with glaze. Serve warm or cool.

Variation: For Maple Chip Ring, double recipe and substitute maple extract for vanilla. Make as directed. Bake in a well-greased twelve-cup fluted tube pan at 350°F for 40 to 45 minutes.

To store baked yeast breads, put them in an airtight container, or wrap them in plastic wrap and keep in a cool place.

Marmalade Lattice Coffee Cake

9 servings

DOUGH

½ cup milk
1 package active dry yeast
6 tablespoons butter
3 tablespoons granulated sugar

¼ teaspoon salt
1 egg, at room temperature
1 egg yolk, at room
   temperature
2 cups all-purpose flour

FILLING

½ cup marmalade
¼ cup butter, softened
¼ cup granulated sugar

¼ cup blanched almonds,
   chopped
⅓ cup mini chocolate chips

TOPPING

½ cup reserved dough
1 egg white

1 teaspoon water

Generously grease a 9-inch square pan. For dough, heat milk to lukewarm (105° to 115°F) in a small saucepan over low heat. Add yeast, stirring until dissolved; set aside. Cream together butter, sugar, and salt in a mixing bowl on medium speed. Add egg and egg yolk, blending well. Alternately mix in flour with yeast mixture with a spoon. *Do not overbeat.* Set aside ½ cup dough for topping; spread remaining dough into prepared pan.

For filling, combine marmalade, butter, sugar, and chopped almonds in a small bowl. Spread filling over dough in pan, spreading to edges. Sprinkle with mini chocolate chips.

For topping roll dough out to a 9 × 4-inch rectangle on a floured surface. Cut rectangle into eight 9 × ½-inch strips. Weave a lattice pattern over filling. Beat together egg white and water with a fork; brush over lattice topping. Cover pan, and put in a warm, draft-free place. Allow dough to double in bulk, about 1 hour.

Preheat oven to 375°F. Bake for 25 to 30 minutes or until golden. Serve from pan, warm or cool.

Mocha Chip Coffee Cake

---

10 servings

MOCHA CHIP TOPPING
½ cup all-purpose flour
½ cup granulated sugar
1 tablespoon instant coffee
½ cup butter, softened

1 teaspoon vanilla
½ cup nuts, chopped
½ cup semisweet chocolate chips

DOUGH
½ cup butter
⅓ cup granulated sugar
Dash of salt
¾ cup milk
2 envelopes active dry yeast

¼ cup lukewarm (105° to 115°F) water
3 eggs, at room temperature
3½ cups all-purpose flour, sifted
½ cup mini chocolate chips

For mocha chip topping, toss together flour, sugar, and instant coffee in a bowl. Cut in butter with a pastry blender or two knives used scissor-fashion until mixture resembles coarse crumbs. Stir in vanilla, chopped nuts, and chocolate chips, mixing well. Set aside.

Generously grease a 10-inch tube pan. For dough, place butter, sugar, and salt in a large mixing bowl. Scald milk in a small saucepan over medium heat. Pour scalded milk over mixture in bowl; stir to melt butter. Cool to room temperature.

Soften yeast in lukewarm water in a small bowl. Stir yeast into cooled milk mixture. Add eggs one at a time and 1½ cups sifted flour on low speed, beating until smooth. Increase speed to medium, and beat for 2 minutes. Lower speed, and add remaining flour, blending well. Stir in mini chocolate chips with a spoon. Turn dough into prepared tube pan. Sprinkle dough with mocha chip topping. Cover with a clean dish towel. Let dough rise in a warm, draft-free place until double, about 1 hour.

Preheat oven to 375°F. Bake coffee cake for 35 to 40 minutes or until golden. Immediately upon removing from oven, turn coffee cake out of pan onto wire rack. Cool.

Banana Chip Muffins

1 dozen

1 cup chopped bananas (approximately 1 medium banana)	1 egg, beaten
	¾ cup milk
	⅓ cup oil
1 teaspoon lemon juice	¼ cup nuts, chopped
1¾ cups all-purpose flour, sifted	½ cup mini chocolate chips
	2 tablespoons granulated sugar
¼ cup granulated sugar	1 teaspoon cinnamon
2½ teaspoons baking powder	

Line twelve muffin tins. Preheat oven to 400°F. Toss chopped bananas with lemon juice; set aside. Stir together sifted flour, ¼ cup sugar, and baking powder in a bowl. Combine beaten egg, milk, and oil in a small bowl. Mix liquid ingredients into dry ingredients, stirring until just moistened. Drain bananas. Fold bananas, chopped nuts, and mini chocolate chips into batter. Fill prepared muffin tins two-thirds full. Mix together 2 tablespoons sugar and cinnamon, and sprinkle onto muffins. Bake for 25 to 30 minutes or until a cake tester inserted in center comes out clean. Cool in tins for 10 minutes; then turn muffins out onto wire rack. Serve warm or cool.

Variation: For Quick Banana Coffee Cake, grease a 9-inch square pan. Pour batter into prepared pan; sprinkle sugar and cinnamon over top. Bake for 20 minutes, or until cake tester inserted in center comes out clean.

Chocolate Chip Oatmeal Muffins

1 dozen

1 cup oatmeal	*3 teaspoons baking powder*
1 cup milk	*1 egg, beaten*
1 cup all-purpose flour, sifted	*¼ cup oil*
⅓ cup granulated sugar	*½ cup mini chocolate chips*

Combine oatmeal and milk; let stand for 20 minutes.
Line twelve muffin tins. Preheat oven to 425°F. Stir together sifted flour, sugar, and baking powder in a bowl. Combine beaten egg, oil, and oatmeal mixture in a small bowl. Add liquid mixture to dry ingredients; stir until just moistened. Fold in mini chocolate chips. Fill prepared muffin tins two-thirds full. Bake for 20 to 25 minutes or until a cake tester inserted in center comes out clean. Cool in tins for 10 minutes; then turn muffins out onto wire rack. Serve warm or cool.

Peanut Butter Chip Muffins

1½ dozen

2 cups all-purpose flour, sifted	*¼ cup butter, softened*
½ cup granulated sugar	*1 cup milk*
2½ teaspoons baking powder	*2 eggs, beaten*
¾ cup chunky peanut butter	*½ cup mini chocolate chips*

TOPPING
¼ cup raspberry jelly	*½ cup peanuts, chopped*

Line eighteen muffin tins. Preheat oven to 400°F. Stir together sifted flour, sugar, and baking powder in a large bowl. Cut in peanut butter and butter with a pastry blender or two knives used scissor-fashion until mixture resembles coarse crumbs. Add milk and beaten eggs, stirring until just moistened. Fold in mini chocolate chips. Fill prepared muffin tins two-thirds full. Bake for 15 to 17 minutes, or until a cake tester inserted in center comes out clean.

Meanwhile, for topping, melt raspberry jelly in a small saucepan over low heat; keep warm. Immediately upon removing muffins from oven, brush tops with melted jelly; dip tops into chopped peanuts. Serve warm or cool.

Variation: For Peanut Butter Chip Bread, grease a 9 × 5 × 3-inch loaf pan; flour bottom. Pour batter into prepared pan. Bake in a preheated 375°F oven for 1 hour or until cake tester inserted in center comes out clean. (Cover with aluminum foil if the bread browns too quickly.) Cool in pan for 15 minutes; then turn bread out onto wire rack. Brush bread with melted jelly; sprinkle with chopped peanuts. Cool completely.

Muffins freeze well. To reheat, place them in a 350°F oven, and warm for 10 to 15 minutes.

Streusel Pecan Chip Muffins

1 dozen

STREUSEL TOPPING

¼ *cup all-purpose flour, sifted*	½ *teaspoon cinnamon*
¼ *cup granulated sugar*	2 *tablespoons butter, softened*

MUFFINS

2 *tablespoons butter*	1 *teaspoon cinnamon*
2 *tablespoons lard*	½ *cup milk*
1 *cup all-purpose flour, sifted*	1 *egg, beaten*
½ *cup granulated sugar*	¾ *cup pecans, chopped*
1 *teaspoon baking powder*	⅓ *cup mini chocolate chips*

Line twelve muffin tins; set aside. Preheat oven to 375°F. For streusel topping, stir together sifted flour, sugar, and cinnamon in a small bowl. Cut in softened butter with a fork until mixture resembles crumbs; set aside.

For muffins, melt butter and lard in a small heavy saucepan over low heat. Remove from heat. Stir together sifted flour, sugar, baking powder, and cinnamon in a bowl. Stir together milk and beaten egg in another bowl. Mix liquid ingredients and melted mixture into dry ingredients. Fold in chopped pecans and mini chocolate chips. Spoon batter into prepared muffin tins; sprinkle each with streusel topping. Bake for 15 to 20 minutes, or until cake tester inserted in center comes out clean. Cool in tins for 15 minutes; then turn muffins out onto wire rack. Cool completely.

Babas au Rhum

1 dozen

DOUGH

1 package active dry yeast
3 tablespoons warm (105° to
   115°F) water
1 cup all-purpose flour
2 tablespoons granulated sugar

¼ teaspoon salt
2 eggs, at room temperature
¼ cup butter, softened
½ cup all-purpose flour

SYRUP

1½ cups granulated sugar
1½ cups water

½ teaspoon grated lemon peel
½ to 1 cup dark rum

FILLING

1 15-or 16-ounce container
   ricotta cheese
3 tablespoons confectioners'
   sugar

1 teaspoon vanilla
⅓ cup mini chocolate chips

GLAZE

¾ cup apricot preserves,
   melted and strained

Lightly grease twelve miniature baba tins or muffin tins; set aside. For dough, sprinkle yeast over warm water in a mixing bowl, stirring to dissolve. Add 1 cup flour, granulated sugar, and salt. Beat in eggs, one at a time on low speed, blending well after each addition. Increase speed to medium, and beat mixture, occasionally scraping sides of bowl, for 4 minutes. Lower speed, and add butter; beat for 2 minutes longer. Add ½ cup flour, beating until smooth (batter will be thick and elastic). Spoon about 1 heaping tablespoon dough into each prepared tin. Cover and set in a warm, draft-free place. Allow dough to rise until double, about 1 hour.

Meanwhile, for syrup, combine granulated sugar, water, and lemon peel in a 2-quart heavy saucepan over medium heat. Cook, stirring constantly, until sugar dissolves. Bring mixture to a boil; boil for 15 minutes without stirring. Remove from heat; stir in rum. Set aside.

Preheat oven to 375°F. Bake babas for 12 to 15 minutes, or until golden brown. Cool in tins for 5 minutes. Remove babas from tins and place in a 13 × 9 × 2-inch pan. With a skewer, prick bottoms and sides of babas. Pour syrup over warm babas; let stand for 2 hours, occasionally basting with syrup. When babas have absorbed the syrup, place them on a wire rack set over a jelly roll pan. Drain for 30 minutes.

Meanwhile, for filling, stir together ricotta cheese, confectioners' sugar, and vanilla in a bowl blending well. Stir in mini chocolate chips; set aside.

Brush drained babas with melted and strained apricot preserves.

To assemble, cut babas in half horizontally. Fill each with 1 heaping tablespoon filling. Serve immediately.

Note: Store leftover Babas au Rhum in refrigerator. Be sure to cover them.

PB & J Rolls

---

1 dozen

BASIC SWEET YEAST DOUGH
1½ cups all-purpose flour   *2 tablespoons butter*
¼ cup granulated sugar   *1 egg, beaten*

1 package active dry yeast   1 cup all-purpose flour
⅔ cup milk   ½ cup all-purpose flour

FILLING
2 tablespoons butter, melted   ½ cup peanuts, chopped
¾ cup peanut butter   ½ cup semisweet chocolate
⅓ cup jam.   chips

Generously grease a large bowl; set aside. For dough stir together
1½ cups flour, sugar, and yeast in a large mixing bowl. Heat milk
with butter in a small heavy saucepan over medium heat until mixture reaches 115°F. Slowly beat warmed milk into flour mixture
with an electric mixer on low speed until well blended. Increase
speed to medium, and beat for 2 minutes. Add beaten egg. Beat in
1 cup flour with a spoon until smooth. Mix in enough of ½ cup
flour to make soft dough. Turn dough onto a lightly floured surface,
and knead for about 10 minutes, or until smooth and elastic. Place
dough in prepared bowl, turning once to grease top. Let dough rise
in a warm, draft-free place until double, about 1½ hours.
Grease a 13 × 9 × 2-inch pan; set aside. Punch dough down. Roll
dough out to a 17 × 12-inch rectangle on a lightly floured surface.
For filling, brush surface of dough with melted butter; then spread
with peanut butter and jam; sprinkle with chopped peanuts and
chocolate chips. Starting with the larger end, roll up dough jelly roll
fashion. Cut into twelve equal rolls. Arrange rolls, cut sides up, in
prepared pan. Cover and let rise in a warm, draft-free place until
double, about 1 hour.
Preheat oven to 375°F. Bake for 25 to 30 minutes, or until lightly
browned. PB & J Rolls may be served warm or cool.

An easy method for slicing rolls uses a piece of ordinary string.
Measure the desired size, and place the string under the roll. Pull
the string up the sides of the roll, cross over the top, and gently
pull until the string cuts through.

Glazed Cheesecake Chip Rolls

---

1 dozen

DOUGH

1 Basic Sweet Yeast Dough,   2 tablespoons butter, melted
  page 54

FILLING

1 3-ounce package cream   1 teaspoon lemon juice
  cheese, softened   ¼ teaspoon vanilla
¼ cup sour cream   1 egg white
2 tablespoons granulated sugar   ½ cup semisweet chocolate
1 tablespoon flour   chips

GLAZE

2 cups confectioners' sugar   ½ teaspoon vanilla
1 tablespoon butter, softened   3 to 5 tablespoons milk

Prepare Basic Sweet Yeast Dough; let rise.

Grease two cookie sheets; set aside. Punch dough down. With floured hands, divide dough into twelve equal pieces; shape each into a smooth ball. Place balls 3 inches apart on prepared cookie sheet; brush with melted butter. Cover cookie sheets, and allow dough to double, about 1 hour.

Meanwhile, for filling, beat together cream cheese, sour cream, granulated sugar, flour, lemon juice, vanilla, and egg white in a small mixing bowl on low speed until smooth. With thumb, make a 1½-inch indentation in center of each roll, forming a cup. Place 5 or 6 chocolate chips in bottom of each cup; fill with 1 tablespoon cream cheese mixture.

Preheat oven to 375°F. Bake for 10 to 15 minutes, or until lightly golden brown. Immediately remove from pans. Cool for 15 minutes.

For glaze, beat together sifted confectioners' sugar, butter, vanilla, and milk in a small mixing bowl. Frost warm rolls. Serve warm or cold.

Note: Store in refrigerator.

Orange Chip Rolls

---

1 dozen

DOUGH
1 Basic Sweet Yeast Dough,
  page 54

FILLING
3 tablespoons granulated sugar   *2 tablespoons butter, softened*
2 teaspoons grated orange peel   *½ cup semisweet chocolate*
                                      chips

ORANGE GLAZE
½ cup confectioners' sugar,   *⅔ teaspoon grated orange peel*
  sifted   *3½ teaspoons orange juice*

Prepare Basic Sweet Dough; let rise.

For filling, toss together granulated sugar and orange peel in a small bowl; set aside. Grease a 13 × 9 × 2-inch pan; set aside. Punch dough down. Roll dough out to a 17 × 12-inch rectangle on a lightly floured surface. Spread with softened butter. Sprinkle dough first with sugar mixture, then with chocolate chips. Starting with longer side, roll dough up jelly roll fashion. Cut roll into twelve slices. Arrange rolls, cut sides up, in prepared pan. Cover and let rise in a warm, draft-free place until double, about 1 hour.

Preheat oven to 375°F. Bake for 12 to 15 minutes, or until lightly golden brown. Cool in pan for 10 minutes; then turn rolls out onto serving plate. Serve warm or cool.

For orange glaze, beat together sifted confectioners' sugar, orange peel, and orange juice in a bowl until smooth. Spread over warm rolls.

Chocolate-Filled Croissants

32 pastries

DOUGH

1 6-ounce cube compressed
  fresh yeast, crumbled
1 cup milk
2 tablespoons granulated sugar
¾ teaspoon salt

1 tablespoon butter, softened
2½ cups bread (not all-purpose)
  flour
1 cup butter, cold

FILLING

2 cups semisweet chocolate
  chips

GLAZE

1 egg, beaten

1 tablespoon milk

For dough, combine crumbled yeast and milk in a large mixing bowl. Add sugar, salt, and 1 tablespoon softened butter. Add flour, ½ cup at a time on low speed, blending well. Knead dough on a lightly floured surface until smooth. Roll dough out to a rectangle three times long as it is wide (about 30 × 10 inches). Mentally divide rectangle into lower, middle, and upper thirds (three 10 × 10-inch sections); lightly mark off sections with fingertip. Cut 1 cup cold butter into ten pieces. With floured hands (flour as often as necessary to prevent butter from sticking), press pieces of butter between palms into flat shapes about the size of silver dollars. Cover lower two-thirds of rectangle with butter pieces, leaving a 1-inch border around edges. Fold down top, or unbuttered third, of rectangle over buttered middle third. Fold bottom third up over top. (The dough should be folded like a business letter; there should now be three layers.) Use fingers to square corners and even all edges. Roll dough out again into a 30 × 10-inch rectangle. Again, fold rectangle into thirds. Wrap dough in plastic wrap. Refrigerate for 30 minutes. Repeat rolling and folding procedure; refrigerate for an additional

20 minutes. Once again, repeat rolling and folding procedure; refrigerate for 6 hours.

Divide chilled dough into four equal pieces. Return three of the pieces to refrigerator. Roll out remaining piece of dough on a lightly floured surface to a rectangle slightly larger than 12 × 10 inches. Using a pastry wheel or a sharp knife, trim dough to exactly 12 × 10 inches. Divide dough into eight 6 × 2¼-inch rectangles. Sprinkle 1 tablespoon chocolate chips across each rectangle, leaving a 1-inch border at each short end. Starting with short ends, roll each rectangle jelly roll fashion around chocolate (do not seal ends of rolls). Arrange rolls, seam sides down, 3 inches apart on an ungreased cookie sheet. Repeat procedure with remaining dough.

For glaze, stir together beaten egg and milk in a small bowl. Brush rolls with glaze. Place uncovered rolls in a warm, draft-free place until double, about 1½ hours. Brush rolls with glaze once during rising.

Preheat oven to 450°F. Brush rolls with glaze. To decorate, use a sharp knife to cut several ⅛-inch-deep diagonal lines across top of each roll. Bake for 15 to 20 minutes, or until golden brown. Immediately remove rolls from cookie sheet. Cool on wire racks. Serve Chocolate-Filled Croissants at room temperature.

Note: If dough is not going to be used within 6 hours, freeze it until ready to use.

Chocolate Chip Cakes

What is a celebration without a cake? What is a cake without chocolate chips? Try the recipes that follow, and bask in applause. Throughout this chapter there are layer cakes chockfull of chips, blended with the flavors of banana, cherry, orange, and peanut butter, to name only a few. Special treats are provided with fluted tube cakes or cupcakes filled with chocolate chips. Melted chips create smooth frostings and creamy fillings that make simple cakes spectacular. When it comes to the marriage of chocolate chips and cakes, the possibilities are endless. Turn the page and see.

CAKES

Cake Servings Table

This table will help you determine the number of servings you can get from a given cake.

Size of Cake	Servings
two 8-inch layers	10 to 14
two 9-inch layers	12 to 16
one 13 × 9 × 2-inch oblong	12 to 15
one 10-inch tube	12 to 16
one 12-cup fluted tube	12 to 16

Frosting Table

This table will help you determine the approximate amount of frosting you need to frost a given cake.

Size of Cake	Amount of Frosting
two 8-inch layers	2¼ cups
two 9-inch layers	2⅔ cups
one 13 × 9 × 2-inch oblong	2½ cups
one 10-inch tube	3 cups
two dozen cupcakes	2⅓ cups

Cherry Chip Quick Cake

Makes two 8-inch layers

2¼ cups cake flour, sifted
3 teaspoons baking powder
½ cup butter, softened
1⅓ cups granulated sugar
¼ cup maraschino cherry juice
½ cup milk

4 egg whites, at room
   temperature
½ cup maraschino cherries,
   drained and chopped
½ cup walnuts, chopped fine
½ cup semisweet chocolate
   chips, chopped

Grease two 8-inch round pans; line bottoms with wax paper. Preheat oven to 350°F. Stir together sifted cake flour and baking powder in a bowl. Cream butter and sugar in a large mixing bowl on medium speed until light and fluffy. Blend in maraschino cherry juice. Lower speed, and alternately add flour mixture with milk. Increase speed to high, and beat for 2 minutes. Add egg whites, and beat for 2 minutes longer. Fold in chopped maraschino cherries, walnuts, and chopped chocolate chips with a spoon. Pour batter into prepared pans. Bake for 30 to 35 minutes, or until cake springs back when lightly touched. Cool in pans for 10 minutes; then turn cakes out onto wire racks; peel off wax paper. Cool completely. Frosting suggestion: Chocolate Cherry Frosting, page 85.

Variation: For Cherry-Covered Chocolate Cupcakes, line twenty-four muffin tins; set aside. Melt ¾ cup semisweet chocolate chips in top of a double boiler over simmering water, stirring until smooth. Remove from heat; set aside. Prepare cake batter as directed. Fill prepared tins half full. Spoon a teaspoon of melted chocolate chips into center of each cupcake; top with remaining batter. Bake for 20 to 25 minutes or until cake springs back lightly when touched. Cool in tins for 15 minutes; then turn cupcakes out onto wire racks. Cool completely.

Chocolate Mint Cake

Makes two 9-inch layers

⅔ cup semisweet chocolate
   chips
¼ cup water
2¼ cups all-purpose flour
½ teaspoon baking powder
1½ teaspoons baking soda

½ cup butter, softened
1¼ cups granulated sugar
3 eggs, at room temperature
¾ teaspoon mint extract
1 cup buttermilk or sour milk

Grease and flour two 9-inch round pans; set aside. Preheat oven to 350°F. Melt chocolate chips with water in top of a double boiler over simmering water, stirring until smooth. Remove from heat. Stir together flour, baking powder, and baking soda in a bowl. Cream butter and sugar in a large mixing bowl on medium speed until light and fluffy. Add eggs, one at a time, blending well after each addition. Add mint extract and melted chocolate mixture. Lower speed, and alternately add flour mixture with buttermilk; blend well. Pour batter into prepared pans. Bake for 25 to 30 minutes, or until cake tester inserted in center comes out clean. Cool in pans for 10 minutes; then turn cakes out onto wire racks. Cool completely. Frosting suggestion: Chocolate Mint Frosting, page 85.

Variations: Instead of mint extract, add either 4 teaspoons instant coffee or 2 tablespoons grated orange peel.

    Also, for cupcakes, line twenty-four to twenty-eight muffin tins; set aside. Prepare cake batter as directed. Fill prepared tins two-thirds to three-quarters full. Bake for 15 to 20 minutes or until a cake tester inserted in center comes out clean. Cool in tins for 15 minutes; then turn cupcakes out on wire racks. Cool completely.

Cocoa Chip Cake

Makes two 9-inch layers

1¾ cups all-purpose flour
¾ cup unsweetened cocoa
1½ teaspoons baking soda
⅔ cup butter
1¾ cups granulated sugar

2 eggs, at room temperature
1 teaspoon vanilla
1½ cups sour cream
⅔ cup mini chocolate chips

Grease and flour two 9-inch round pans; set aside. Preheat oven to 350°F. Stir together flour, cocoa, and baking soda in a bowl. Cream butter and sugar in a large mixing bowl on medium speed until light and fluffy. Beat in eggs one at a time, blending well after each addition, and add vanilla. Lower speed, and alternately add flour mixture with sour cream, blending well. Stir in mini chocolate chips with a spoon. Spread batter into prepared pans. Bake for 30 to 35 minutes, or until cake tester inserted in center comes out clean. Cool in pans for 10 minutes; then turn cakes out onto wire racks. Cool completely.

Variations: For Orange Cheesecake Cups, line twenty-eight muffin tins; set aside. For orange cheesecake filling, beat together 1 8-ounce package softened cream cheese, 1 egg, ⅓ cup sugar, and 1 tablespoon all-purpose flour in a small mixing bowl on medium speed until smooth. Stir in 1 tablespoon grated orange peel with a spoon. Set aside. Prepare cake batter as directed. Fill prepared tins half full. Spoon 1 teaspoon filling into center of each cupcake; top with 1 teaspoon remaining batter. Bake for 25 minutes or until cupcake springs back when lightly touched. Cool in tins for 15 minutes; then turn cupcakes out onto wire rack. Cool completely. Store Orange Cheesecake Cups in refrigerator.

Devilish Devil's Food Cake

Makes two 9-inch layers

½ cup semisweet chocolate chips
1 1-ounce square unsweetened chocolate
2 cups cake flour, sifted
1 teaspoon baking soda
½ cup butter, softened

2 cups brown sugar, packed firm
2 eggs, at room temperature
1 teaspoon vanilla
1 cup buttermilk or sour milk
½ teaspoon red food coloring

Grease two 9-inch round pans; line bottoms with wax paper. Preheat oven to 350°F. Melt chocolates in top of a double boiler over simmering water, stirring until smooth. Remove from heat. Stir together sifted cake flour and baking soda in a bowl. Cream butter and brown sugar in a large mixing bowl on medium speed until fluffy. Add eggs, one at a time, blending well after each addition. Add vanilla. Lower speed, and alternately add flour mixture with buttermilk, blending well. Add red food coloring. Increase speed to medium, and beat for 2 minutes. Pour batter into prepared pans. Bake for 25 to 30 minutes, or until cake tester inserted in center comes out clean. Cool in pans for 10 minutes; then turn cakes out onto wire racks; peel off wax paper. Cool completely.

Variation: For Devilish Devil's Food Sheet Cake, grease and flour a 13 × 9 × 2-inch pan. Prepare cake batter as directed. Bake for 25 to 30 minutes or until cake tester inserted in center comes out clean.

Liquid ingredients usually should be added alternately with dry ingredients, beginning and ending with the dry.

Peanut Better Cake

2¼ cups cake flour, sifted
3 teaspoons baking powder
⅓ cup butter, softened
1½ cups granulated sugar
⅓ cup chunky peanut butter

2 eggs, at room temperature
1 teaspoon vanilla
1 cup milk
½ cup semisweet chocolate
chips, chopped finely

Grease two 9-inch round pans; line bottoms with wax paper. Preheat oven to 375°F. Stir together sifted cake flour and baking powder in a bowl. Cream butter and sugar in a large mixing bowl on medium speed until light and fluffy. Beat in peanut butter. Add eggs, one at a time, blending well after each addition. Add vanilla. Lower speed, and alternately add flour mixture with milk; blend well. Fold chopped chocolate chips into batter. Pour batter into prepared pans. Bake for 25 minutes, or until cake tester inserted in center comes out clean. Cool in pans for 15 minutes; then turn cakes out onto wire racks; peel off wax paper. Cool completely. Frosting suggestion: Chocolate Peanut Better Frosting, page 86.

Speckled Banana Cake

Makes two 9-inch layers

¼ cup cake flour
⅔ cup nuts, chopped fine
½ cup semisweet chocolate
chips, chopped fine
2 cups cake flour
1¼ teaspoons baking powder

1¼ teaspoons baking soda
⅔ cup butter, softened
1⅔ cups granulated sugar
3 eggs, at room temperature
⅔ cup buttermilk
1¼ cups mashed bananas

Grease two 9-inch round pans; line bottoms with wax paper. Preheat oven to 350°F. Toss together ¼ cup cake flour with chopped nuts and chocolate chips in a small bowl; set aside. Stir together 2 cups cake flour, baking powder, and baking soda in another bowl. Cream butter and sugar in a large mixing bowl on medium speed until light and fluffy. Add eggs, one at a time, blending well after each addition. Lower speed, and alternately add flour mixture with buttermilk. Blend in mashed bananas. Increase speed to high, and beat for 3 minutes. Fold in chopped nuts and chocolate chip mixture with a spoon. Pour batter into prepared pans. Bake for 35 to 40 minutes, or until cake tester inserted in center comes out clean. Cool in pans for 15 minutes. Then turn cakes out onto wire racks; peel off wax paper. Cool completely.

Variation: For cupcakes, line twenty-eight muffin tins; set aside. Prepare cake batter as directed. Fill prepared tins two-thirds full. Bake for 15 to 20 minutes, or until a cake tester inserted in center comes out clean. Cool in tins for 15 minutes; then turn cupcakes out onto wire racks. Cool completely. Frost if desired.

Yummy Mocha Cups

Makes 1 dozen

CUPCAKES

*1 1-ounce square unsweetened
    chocolate
1 cup all-purpose flour
1 teaspoon baking powder
¼ teaspoon baking soda
1 tablespoon instant coffee*

*½ cup milk
6 tablespoons butter, softened
½ cup granulated sugar
1 egg, at room temperature
1 egg yolk, at room
    temperature*

TOPPING

*1 egg white, at room
    temperature
1 teaspoon instant coffee*

*⅓ cup granulated sugar
½ cup nuts, chopped
½ cup mini chocolate chips*

Line twelve muffin tins; set aside. Preheat oven to 350°F. For cupcakes, melt unsweetened chocolate in a measuring cup set in simmering water, stirring until smooth; remove from heat. Stir together flour, baking powder, and baking soda in a bowl. Dissolve instant coffee in milk in a cup. Cream butter and sugar in a mixing bowl on medium speed until light and fluffy. Add egg and egg yolk. Lower speed, and alternately add flour mixture with coffee mixture, blending well. Blend in melted chocolate. Fill prepared tins two-thirds full with batter. Bake for 12 minutes.

Meanwhile, for topping, beat egg white and instant coffee in a small mixing bowl until foamy. Gradually add sugar, beating until stiff peaks form. Gently fold in chopped nuts and mini chocolate chips. Immediately upon removing from oven, spoon 1 teaspoon topping onto each cupcake. Return to oven, and bake for 10 to 12 minutes longer. Cool in tins for 15 minutes; then turn cupcakes out onto wire racks. Cool completely.

To freeze cupcakes, place them on a cookie sheet in freezer until hard. Transfer frozen cupcakes to plastic bags. To thaw, keep cupcakes at room temperature for 30 minutes.

Almond Chocolate Chip Cake

Makes 10 servings

1¼ cups all-purpose flour,
    sifted
2 teaspoons baking powder
1½ cups whipping cream
1 cup granulated sugar
½ teaspoon almond extract

3 eggs, at room temperature
¼ cup granulated sugar
1 cup blanched almonds,
    chopped fine
1 cup mini chocolate chips
6 tablespoons amaretto liqueur

FROSTING
2½ cups confectioners' sugar
1 cup unsweetened cocoa
½ cup butter, softened

6 tablespoons milk
½ teaspoon almond extract

Grease two 8- or 9-inch round pans; line bottoms with wax paper; then grease paper, and dust with flour. Preheat oven to 350°F. Stir together sifted flour and baking powder in a bowl; set aside.

Beat cream in a large mixing bowl until thick. Gradually add 1 cup granulated sugar, beating until soft peaks form. Beat eggs in a small mixing bowl on medium speed. Slowly add ¼ cup granulated sugar, beating until mixture is thick and lemon-colored. Add almond extract into egg mixture. Fold eggs into whipped cream mixture. Now fold in flour mixture, blending well. Fold in chopped almonds and mini chocolate chips. Spread batter in prepared pans. Bake for 30 minutes, or until cake tester inserted in center comes out clean. Cool in pans for 10 minutes; then turn cakes out onto wire racks; peel off wax paper. Cool completely. Brush cooled cakes with amaretto.

For frosting stir together confectioners' sugar and cocoa in a bowl. Cream butter in a small mixing bowl on medium speed until light. Lower speed, and alternately add cocoa mixture with milk, beating until smooth. Add almond extract; blend well.

To assemble cake, place one layer, amaretto side up, on serving plate; spread with about ¾ cup frosting. Top with remaining layer, amaretto side up, and frost top and sides of cake.

When baking layer cakes, do not allow pans to touch.

Billyburg Orange Cake

Makes 10 servings

¼ cup cake flour
1 cup golden raisins, chopped
½ cup walnuts, chopped fine
½ cup semisweet chocolate
    chips, chopped fine
2½ cups cake flour
1½ teaspoons baking soda

ORANGE BUTTER FROSTING
⅓ cup butter, softened
3 cups confectioners' sugar

¾ cup butter, softened
1½ cups granulated sugar
3 eggs at room temperature
1½ teaspoons vanilla
1½ cups buttermilk
1 tablespoon grated orange peel

3 to 4 tablespoons orange
    liqueur
2 teaspoons grated orange peel

Grease two 9-inch round pans; line bottoms with wax paper. Preheat oven to 350°F. Toss together ¼ cup cake flour with chopped raisins, walnuts, and chocolate chips in a small bowl; set aside. Stir together 2½ cups cake flour and baking soda in another bowl. Cream butter and granulated sugar in a large mixing bowl on medium speed until light and fluffy. Add eggs, one at a time, blending well after each addition. Add vanilla. Lower speed, and alternately add flour mixture with buttermilk. Increase speed to high, and beat mixture for 3 minutes. Stir in chopped raisins, walnuts, and chocolate chip mixture and orange peel with a spoon. Pour batter into prepared pans. Bake for 30 to 35 minutes, or until cake tester inserted in center comes out clean. Cool in pans for 15 minutes; then turn cakes out onto wire racks; peel off wax paper. Cool completely.

For orange butter frosting, beat together butter, confectioners' sugar, and orange liqueur in a small mixing bowl until smooth. Stir in orange peel with a spoon. Frost cooled cake.

Note: Billyburg Orange Cake may be prepared in a 13 × 9 × 2-inch pan if desired. Increase baking time to 40 to 45 minutes.

Store cakes with whipped cream fillings in the refrigerator.

Black Forest Cake

Makes 10 servings

CHERRY FILLING
3 16-ounce cans pitted tart
    cherries, drained (reserve
    juice)

½ cup kirsch

CAKE
⅔ cup semisweet chocolate
    chips
½ cup butter, softened

¾ cup ground blanched
    almonds
¾ cup all-purpose flour, sifted

½ cup granulated sugar
4 eggs, at room temperature

1 teaspoon baking powder

CHERRY TOPPING
2 tablespoons granulated sugar
2 tablespoons cornstarch
1 tablespoon reserved cherry
   juice

½ teaspoon almond extract
¼ teaspoon red food coloring
1 cup cherries

WHIPPED CREAM FILLING AND TOPPING
3 cups whipping cream
½ cup confectioners' sugar

2 tablespoons kirsch (optional)

For cherry filling, soak cherries in kirsch in a bowl; set aside.

For cake, grease two 8-inch round pans; line bottoms with wax paper. Preheat oven to 350°F. Melt chocolate chips in top of a double boiler over simmering water, stirring until smooth; remove from heat. Cream butter and granulated sugar in a large mixing bowl on medium speed until light and fluffy. Add eggs, one at a time, blending well after each addition. Blend in ground almonds and melted chocolate chips. Lower speed, and add sifted flour and baking powder; blend well. Spread batter in prepared pans. Bake for 20 to 25 minutes, or until cake tester inserted in center comes out clean. Cool in pans for 10 minutes; then turn cakes out onto wire racks; peel off wax paper. Cool completely.

Drain cherries; reserve kirsch. For cherry topping, combine granulated sugar and cornstarch in a bowl, stir in 1 tablespoon reserved cherry juice, almond extract, and red food coloring. Add 1 cup drained cherries, stirring to coat. Let mixture stand for 1 hour.

Strain cherries, pouring liquid into small heavy saucepan. Cook, stirring constantly, until mixture becomes very thick. (When the cherries are added, the mixture will thin out.) Fold in cherries with a rubber spatula, and cook, stirring occasionally, until mixture is once again thick. Remove from heat; cool completely.

For whipped cream filling and topping, beat whipping cream, confectioners' sugar, and kirsch in chilled bowl with clean, chilled beaters until stiff; reserve 1 cup for garnish.

To assemble cake, cut layers in half horizontally; sprinkle with reserved kirsch. Place one layer, kirsch side up, on serving plate. Spread with about ¾ cup whipped cream. Arrange one-third of drained cherries on filling, and cover with second layer. Repeat procedure, ending with fourth layer. Frost top and sides of cake with remaining whipped cream. Pipe whipped cream rosettes around top edge of cake. Spoon cherry topping onto center of cake. Chill until ready to serve.

To cut a cake layer in half, place toothpicks around the center of the sides as a guide. With a sharp knife, carefully cut layer, using a light sawing motion.

Chocolate Oatmeal Cake

Makes one 13 × 9 × 2-inch layer

⅔ cup semisweet chocolate chips	½ cup butter, softened
1 cup oatmeal	1 cup granulated sugar
1¼ cups boiling water	1 cup brown sugar, packed firm
1½ cups all-purpose flour	3 eggs, at room temperature
1 teaspoon baking soda	1 teaspoon vanilla

TOPPING

6 tablespoons butter, softened	¼ cup milk
1 cup brown sugar, packed firm	2 cups flaked coconut

Toss together chocolate chips and oatmeal in a bowl. Pour boiling water over mixture; let stand for 20 minutes. Stir to blend before using.

Grease and flour a 13 × 9 × 2-inch pan. Preheat oven to 350°F. Stir together flour and baking soda in a bowl. Cream butter and sugars in a large mixing bowl on medium speed until light and fluffy. Add eggs, one at a time, blending well after each addition.

Add vanilla. Lower speed, and alternately add flour mixture with oatmeal mixture; blend well. Pour batter into prepared pan. Bake for 35 to 40 minutes, or until cake tester inserted in center comes out clean.

Meanwhile, for topping cream together butter and brown sugar in a small mixing bowl on medium speed. Blend in milk. Stir in coconut with a spoon. Immediately upon removing cake from oven, spread topping over cake. Return to oven, and broil 4 inches from heat for about 4 minutes. Serve cake warm or cool.

Variation: For a tasty variation, add 1 teaspoon rum extract and 1 tablespoon grated orange peel instead of vanilla to cake batter.

Double Chocolate Chip Cake

Makes one 13 × 9-inch layer

2 cups all-purpose flour, sifted
1 teaspoon baking powder
1 teaspoon baking soda
1 cup butter, softened
1⅓ cups granulated sugar
3 eggs, at room temperature

1 teaspoon vanilla
1 cup milk
2 1-ounce squares unsweetened
  chocolate, grated
1 cup mini chocolate chips

Grease a 13 × 9 × 2-inch pan; flour bottom. Preheat oven to 350°F. Stir together sifted flour, baking powder, and baking soda in a bowl. Cream butter and sugar in a large mixing bowl on medium speed until light and fluffy. Add eggs, one at a time, blending well after each addition. Add vanilla. Lower speed, and alternately add flour mixture with milk; blend well. Fold in grated unsweetened chocolate with a spoon. Pour batter into prepared pan; sprinkle with mini chocolate chips. Bake for 35 to 40 minutes, or until cake tester inserted in center comes out clean. Cool on wire rack. Serve cake from pan.

Chocolate Pound Cake

1 loaf

⅔ cup semisweet chocolate
    chips
1⅓ cups all-purpose flour,
    sifted
½ teaspoon baking powder

1 cup butter, softened
1 cup granulated sugar
5 eggs, at room temperature
1½ teaspoons vanilla

Grease a 9 × 5 × 3-inch loaf pan; flour bottom. Preheat oven to 350°F. Melt chocolate chips in top of a double boiler over simmering water, stirring until smooth. Remove from heat; set aside. Stir together sifted flour and baking powder in a bowl. Cream butter and sugar in a large mixing bowl on medium speed until light and fluffy. Add eggs, one at a time, blending well after each addition. Add vanilla. Blend in melted chocolate. Lower speed, and add flour mixture, blending well. Pour batter into prepared pan. Bake for 50 minutes to 1 hour, or until cake tester inserted in center comes out clean. Cool in pan for 10 minutes; then turn cake out onto wire rack. Cool completely.

Dropped Chocolate Cake

1 tube cake

CHOCOLATE SYRUP
1 cup semisweet chocolate chips
2 tablespoons butter

3 tablespoons light corn syrup
3 tablespoons hot water

CAKE
3 cups all-purpose flour
1½ teaspoons baking powder

3 eggs, at room temperature
½ teaspoon vanilla

½ teaspoon baking soda
1 cup butter, softened
1¾ cups granulated sugar

1¼ cups milk
¾ cup chocolate syrup (reserve
   remaining for frosting)

FROSTING
Reserved chocolate syrup
1 cup confectioners' sugar

1 teaspoon vanilla
2 tablespoons milk

For chocolate syrup, melt chocolate chips and butter with corn syrup and hot water in top of a double boiler over simmering water, stirring until smooth. Remove from heat; set aside.

Grease and flour a 10-inch tube pan; set aside. Preheat oven to 350°F. For cake, stir together flour, baking powder, and baking soda in a bowl. Cream butter and granulated sugar in a large mixing bowl on medium speed until light and fluffy. Add eggs, one at a time, blending well after each addition. Add vanilla. Lower speed, and alternately add flour mixture with milk, blending well. Reserve 2 cups of batter. Pour remaining batter into prepared pan. Add ¾ cup chocolate syrup to reserved batter; pour over batter in pan. Bake for 1 hour to 1 hour and 5 minutes, or until cake tester inserted in center comes out clean. Cool in pan for 15 minutes; then turn cake out onto wire rack. Cool completely.

For frosting, beat together reserved syrup, confectioners' sugar, vanilla, and milk in a small mixing bowl on medium speed, until smooth. Frost cooled cake.

Fudge Pecan Cake

1 tube cake

⅓ cup semisweet chocolate
   chips
3 1-ounce squares unsweetened
   chocolate
3⅔ cups all-purpose flour,
   sifted
3½ teaspoons baking powder
½ teaspoon baking soda

¾ cup butter, softened
2 cups granulated sugar
2 eggs, at room temperature
2 teaspoons vanilla
1½ cups buttermilk
1 cup pecans, chopped fine
Sifted confectioners' sugar

Grease and flour a 10-inch tube pan; set aside. Preheat oven to 350°F. Melt chocolate in top of a double boiler over simmering water, stirring until smooth. Remove from heat. Stir together sifted flour, baking powder, and baking soda in a bowl. Cream butter and granulated sugar in a large mixing bowl on medium speed until light and fluffy. Add eggs, one at a time, blending well after each addition. Add vanilla. Alternately stir flour mixture with buttermilk into batter with a spoon; mix well. Blend in melted chocolates. Fold in chopped pecans. Spoon batter into prepared pan. Bake for 1 hour, or until cake tester inserted in center comes out clean. Cool in pan for 15 minutes; then turn cake out onto wire rack. Cool completely. Sprinkle cooled cake with sifted confectioners' sugar.

Chocolate Chip Chiffon Cake

1 tube cake

2¼ cups cake flour, sifted
1 cup granulated sugar
1 tablespoon baking powder
½ cup oil
7 egg yolks
1 teaspoon vanilla
¾ cup water

½ cup semisweet chocolate chips, chopped fine
1 cup (about 8) egg whites, at room temperature
½ cup granulated sugar
½ teaspoon cream of tartar

Preheat oven to 325°F. Stir together sifted cake flour, 1 cup sugar, and baking powder in a large bowl; make a well in center of dry ingredients. Add, in the following order, oil, egg yolks, vanilla, and water. Beat mixture with a wire whisk until smooth. Stir in chopped chocolate chips. Beat egg whites in a large mixing bowl on high speed until foamy. Gradually add ½ cup sugar and cream of tartar, beating until whites form stiff peaks. Pour chocolate chip mixture in a thin stream into beaten egg whites; gently fold until well blended. Pour batter into an ungreased 10-inch tube pan. Bake for 1 hour and 10 minutes, or until cake springs back when lightly touched. Immediately upon removing cake from oven, invert pan. Cool completely.

Note: Immediately upon removing a chiffon cake from the oven, it is important to turn it upside down until cool. This prevents the cake from falling. Invert pan onto a large soda bottle.

Variations: Try dressing up this versatile chiffon cake by adding any one of the following:

MOCHA CHIP CHIFFON CAKE: Add ¾ cup cool strong coffee *instead* of water to dry ingredients.

ORANGE CHIP CHIFFON CAKE: Add ¾ cup orange juice *instead* of water and 2 tablespoons grated orange peel to dry ingredients.

COCOA CHIP CHIFFON CAKE: Reduce sifted cake flour to 1¾ cups. Boil ¾ cup water, and add ½ cup sifted unsweetened cocoa, stirring until smooth; cool to room temperature. Mix cake as directed, except increase sugar added while beating egg whites to ¾ cup. Pour batter into ungreased pan. Bake for 55 minutes to 1 hour and 5 minutes.

Chocolate Almond Cake

1 fluted tube cake

⅔ cup semisweet chocolate
   chips, chopped
1½ cups ground almonds
2½ cups cake flour
1 teaspoon baking soda
3 egg whites, at room
   temperature

⅔ cup butter, softened
1 cup granulated sugar
3 egg yolks
3 tablespoons dark rum
1 cup buttermilk or sour milk

COCOA RUM GLAZE
1 cup confectioners' sugar
2 tablespoons unsweetened
   cocoa
1 tablespoon dark rum

4 to 6 tablespoons milk
¼ cup blanched almonds,
   chopped

    Grease and flour a 12-cup fluted tube pan; set aside. Preheat oven to 350°F. Toss together chopped chocolate chips and ground almonds in a bowl; set aside. Stir together cake flour and baking soda in another bowl. Beat egg whites in a small mixing bowl on high speed until stiff peaks form; set aside. Cream butter and granulated sugar in a large mixing bowl on medium speed until light and fluffy. Add egg yolks, one at a time, blending well after each addition. Blend in rum and chocolate-almond mixture. Lower speed, and alternately add flour mixture with buttermilk. Gently fold in beaten egg whites with a spatula, blending until no white streaks remain. Pour batter into prepared pan. Bake for 40 to 45 minutes, or until cake tester inserted in center comes out clean. Cool in pan for 10 minutes; then turn cake out onto wire rack. Cool completely.

For cocoa rum glaze, beat together confectioners' sugar, cocoa, rum, and milk in a small mixing bowl on medium speed until smooth (more milk may be necessary). Spoon glaze over cooled cake; sprinkle with chopped almonds. Allow glaze to set.

Chocolate Rum Surprise Cake

---

1 fluted tube cake

FILLING

1 cup semisweet chocolate chips	1 3-ounce package cream
¾ cup sweetened condensed	cheese, cut into pieces
milk	1 cup nuts, chopped

CAKE

⅔ cup semisweet chocolate	½ cup butter, softened
chips	1½ cups granulated sugar
2 tablespoons hot water	3 eggs, at room temperature
2 ⅔ cups all-purpose flour	⅓ cup dark rum
2 teaspoons baking powder	1 cup sour cream
½ teaspoon baking soda	Sifted confectioners' sugar

For filling, melt chocolate chips with sweetened condensed milk and cream cheese in a heavy saucepan over low heat, stirring until smooth. Stir in chopped nuts. Remove from heat; cool for 15 minutes.

Grease and flour a 12-cup fluted tube pan; set aside. Preheat oven to 350°F. For cake, melt chocolate chips with hot water in a small heavy saucepan over low heat, stirring until smooth. Remove from heat. Stir together flour, baking powder, and baking soda in a bowl. Cream butter and granulated sugar in a large mixing bowl on medium speed until light and fluffy. Add eggs one at a time, blending well after each addition. Add rum. Lower speed, and alternately add flour mixture with sour cream. Pour about 4 cups batter into prepared pan. Carefully spoon filling over batter without touching sides of pan. Pour remaining batter over filling. Bake for 50 minutes to 1 hour, or until cake springs back when lightly touched. Cool in pan for 45 minutes; then turn cake out onto serving plate. Cool completely. Sprinkle cake with sifted confectioners' sugar.

Variation: Substitute 1 cup flaked coconut for chopped nuts in filling, if preferred.

Do not grease a fluted tube pan with oil. The cake will absorb the oil while baking, causing it to stick to the pan. To grease and flour a fluted tube pan easily, melt 2 tablespoons butter; stir in 4½ teaspoons flour, blending well; paint mixture inside pan with a pastry brush.

Cocoa Apple Spice Cake

1 fluted tube cake

3 cups all-purpose flour
3 tablespoons unsweetened
cocoa
1 teaspoon baking soda
1 teaspoon cinnamon
1 teaspoon nutmeg
1 cup butter, softened
2 cups granulated sugar
3 eggs, at room temperature

2 teaspoons vanilla
¾ cups sour cream
2 cups grated apples
(approximately 3 medium-
sized apples)
1 cup nuts, chopped
¾ cup mini chocolate chips
Sifted confectioners' sugar

Grease and flour a 12-cup fluted tube pan; set aside. Preheat oven to 350°F. Stir together flour, cocoa, baking soda, cinnamon, and nutmeg in a bowl. Cream butter and granulated sugar in a large mixing bowl on medium speed until light and fluffy. Add eggs, one at a time, blending well after each addition. Add vanilla. Lower speed, and alternately add flour mixture with sour cream; blend well. Stir in grated apples, chopped nuts, and mini chocolate chips with a spoon. Spoon batter into prepared pan. Bake for 1 hour to 1 hour and 10 minutes, or until cake tester inserted in center comes out clean. Cool for 10 minutes in pan; then turn cake out onto wire rack. Cool completely. Sprinkle cooled cake with sifted confectioners' sugar.

Note: Cocoa Apple Spice Cake freezes well.

Orange and Chocolate Ribbon Cake

---

1 fluted tube cake

FILLING

1 cup semisweet chocolate chips
½ cup nuts, chopped

⅓ cup sweetened condensed milk

CAKE

2 cups all-purpose flour
1 teaspoon baking powder
¾ cup butter, softened
2 cups granulated sugar

2 eggs, at room temperature
1 teaspoon vanilla
1 cup sour cream
2 tablespoons grated orange peel

GLAZE

½ cup confectioners' sugar, sifted
1 to 2 tablespoons orange liqueur or juice

1 teaspoon grated orange peel

Grease and flour a 12-cup fluted tube pan. Preheat oven to 350°F. For filling, stir together chocolate chips, chopped nuts, and sweetened condensed milk in a bowl. Set aside.

For cake, stir together flour and baking powder in another bowl. Cream butter and granulated sugar in a large mixing bowl on medium speed, until light and fluffy. Add eggs, one at a time, blending well after each addition. Add vanilla. Lower speed, and alternately add flour mixture with sour cream. Add orange peel. Increase speed to medium, and beat for 3 minutes. Pour about 2½ cups batter into prepared pan. Carefully spoon filling over batter without touching sides of pan. Pour remaining batter over filling. Bake for 1 hour and 5 minutes to 1 hour and 20 minutes, or until cake tester inserted in center comes out clean. Cool for 45 minutes in pan; then turn cake out onto serving plate. Cool completely.

For glaze, beat together sifted confectioners' sugar and orange liqueur in a bowl until smooth. Stir in orange peel. Spoon glaze over cooled cake. Allow glaze to set.

Peanut Butter Streusel Cake

1 fluted tube cake

CAKE

½ cup butter, softened	3 eggs, at room temperature
2 cups brown sugar, packed firm	1 teaspoon vanilla
1 cup peanut butter	1 cup milk
2¼ cups all-purpose flour	1 teaspoon baking powder
	½ teaspoon baking soda

STREUSEL

¾ cup semisweet chocolate chips	1 cup reserved crumb mixture

PEANUT BUTTER GLAZE

1 cup confectioners' sugar	2 tablespoons peanut butter
2 tablespoons unsweetened cocoa	½ teaspoon vanilla
	2 to 3 tablespoons milk

Grease and flour a 12-cup fluted tube pan; set aside. Preheat oven to 350°F. For cake, beat together butter, brown sugar, and peanut butter in a large mixing bowl on medium speed until smooth. Lower speed, and add flour, blending until mixture resembles coarse crumbs. Reserve 1 cup crumb mixture for streusel. Add eggs, one at a time, on medium speed to remaining mixture, blending well after each addition. Lower speed, and add milk, baking powder, and baking soda. Increase speed to medium, and beat for 3 minutes.

For streusel, toss chocolate chips with reserved crumb mixture. Pour about 2½ cups batter into prepared pan; sprinkle streusel over batter. Pour remaining batter over streusel. Bake for 55 minutes to 1 hour and 5 minutes, or until cake tester inserted in center comes out clean. Cool in pan for 45 minutes; then turn cake out onto serving plate. Cool completely.

For peanut butter glaze, beat together confectioners' sugar, cocoa, peanut butter, vanilla, and milk in a small mixing bowl on medium speed until smooth. Spoon glaze over cooled cake. Allow glaze to set.

Pumpkin Chip Cake

1 fluted tube cake

2 cups all-purpose flour	1½ cups granulated sugar
1 teaspoon baking powder	3 eggs, at room temperature
1 teaspoon baking soda	1 teaspoon vanilla
1 teaspoon cinnamon	1 cup canned pumpkin
½ teaspoon ginger	⅓ cup sour cream or yogurt
¼ teaspoon cloves	1 cup nuts, chopped
½ cup butter, softened	1 cup semisweet chocolate chips

SPICE GLAZE

1 cup confectioners' sugar	2 to 3 tablespoons milk
1 tablespoon light corn syrup	1 teaspoon nutmeg

Grease and flour a 12-cup fluted tube pan; set aside. Preheat oven to 350°F. Stir together flour, baking powder, baking soda, cinnamon, ginger, and cloves in a bowl. Cream butter and granulated sugar in a large mixing bowl on medium speed until light and fluffy. Add eggs, one at a time, blending well after each addition. Add vanilla. Blend in pumpkin. Lower speed, and alternately add flour mixture with sour cream; blend well. Stir in chopped nuts and chocolate chips with a spoon. Pour batter into prepared pan. Bake for 1 hour and 15 minutes, or until cake tester inserted in center comes out clean. Cool in pan for 15 minutes; then turn cake out onto wire rack. Cool completely.

For spice glaze, beat together confectioners' sugar, corn syrup, milk, and nutmeg in a small mixing bowl on medium speed until smooth. Spoon glaze over cooled cake. Allow glaze to set.

Chocolate Frosting

Frosts tops and sides of two 8- or 9-inch layers

1⅓ cups semisweet chocolate
   chips
3½ cups confectioners' sugar

½ cup butter, softened
½ cup light cream or milk

Melt chocolate chips in top of a double boiler over simmering water, stirring until smooth. Remove from heat. Beat together confectioners' sugar, butter, light cream, and melted chocolate chips in a small mixing bowl on medium speed until smooth. Frost cooled cake.

Variations: Any one of the following may be added to Chocolate Frosting:

CHOCOLATE ALMOND FROSTING
   1 teaspoon almond extract

CHOCOLATE CHERRY FROSTING
   ½ cup maraschino cherries, drained and chopped

CHOCOLATE MINT FROSTING
   ¼ teaspoon mint extract

CHOCOLATE MOCHA FROSTING
   2 teaspoons instant coffee

CHOCOLATE NUT FROSTING
½ cup nuts, chopped fine

CHOCOLATE ORANGE FROSTING
½ teaspoon orange extract
1 teaspoon grated orange peel

CHOCOLATE RUM FROSTING
1 teaspoon rum extract

Chocolate Cream Cheese Frosting

Frosts tops and sides of two 8- or 9-inch layers

⅔ cup semisweet chocolate
    chips
2 tablespoons butter
3 cups confectioners' sugar,
    sifted

1 3-ounce package cream
    cheese, softened
3 tablespoons light cream or
    milk
1 teaspoon vanilla

Melt chocolate chips and butter in top of a double boiler over simmering water, stirring until smooth. Remove from heat. Beat together sifted confectioners' sugar, cream cheese, light cream, vanilla, and melted chocolate mixture in a small mixing bowl on medium speed until smooth. Frost cooled cake.

Chocolate Peanut Better Frosting

Frosts tops and sides of two 8- or 9-inch layers

½ cup semisweet chocolate
    chips

3 cups confectioners' sugar,
    sifted

3 tablespoons butter	¼ cup plus 2 tablespoons milk
½ cup chunky peanut butter	1 teaspoon vanilla

Melt chocolate chips and butter with peanut butter in top of a double boiler over simmering water; stir to blend. Remove from heat. Beat together sifted confectioners' sugar, milk, vanilla, and melted chocolate mixture in a small mixing bowl on medium speed until smooth. (More milk may be added if necessary.) Frost cooled cake.

To assure that frosting will not run off cake, cool cake completely before frosting. Brush away any loose crumbs. To frost a layer cake, place the first layer top side down. The second layer should be frosted top side up.

Chocolate Swirl Frosting

Frosts tops and sides of two 8- or 9-inch layers

¾ cup granulated sugar	¼ teaspoon cream of tartar
¼ cup light corn syrup	Dash of salt
2 tablespoons water	1 teaspoon vanilla
2 egg whites, at room temperature	¼ cup semisweet chocolate chips

Combine sugar, corn syrup, water, egg whites, cream of tartar, and salt in top of a double boiler over simmering water. Beat mixture with a rotary beater for about 7 minutes or until it holds peaks. Remove from heat. Add vanilla, and continue to beat until stiff peaks form. Fold in chocolate chips; let frosting stand for 2 minutes. Frost cooled cake. (Chocolate chips will swirl throughout frosting when spread on cake.)

Chocolate Icing

Frosts 1 tube cake

1 cup semisweet chocolate chips   2 cups confectioners' sugar,
⅓ cup evaporated milk   sifted

   Melt chocolate chips in top of a double boiler over simmering water, stirring until smooth. Remove from heat; blend in evaporated milk. Beat in sifted confectioners' sugar, blending until smooth. (More evaporated milk may be added if necessary.) Frost cooled cake.

Chocolate Rum Filling

Makes about 5 cups

1⅔ cups semisweet chocolate   2 tablespoons dark rum
   chips
2 cups whipping cream

   Melt chocolate chips with whipping cream in a 2-quart heavy saucepan over low heat, stirring until smooth. Transfer chocolate mixture to a small mixing bowl. Stir in rum. Cool for 15 minutes. Chill mixture for 1 to 2 hours.
   Beat chilled mixture on medium speed until thick and stiff. Spread filling between cooled cake layers.

Note: Chocolate Rum Filling is a great filling for a jelly roll cake.

Whipped Cream Filling

Makes about 1½ cups

½ cup whipping cream   *½ teaspoon vanilla*
2 tablespoons confectioners'   *½ cup mini chocolate chips*
* sugar, sifted*

Beat whipping cream, sifted confectioners' sugar, and vanilla in a chilled small mixing bowl with chilled beaters until stiff. Fold in mini chocolate chips with a spoon. Spread filling between cooled cake layers.

Variations: Any one of the following flavorings may be used:

COCOA CHIP CREAM
  1 tablespoon unsweetened cocoa

CRÈME DE CACAO CHIP CREAM
  Omit confectioners' sugar and vanilla
  Add 1 tablespoon plus 1½ teaspoons crème de cacao liqueur

CRÈME DE MENTHE CHIP CREAM
  Omit vanilla and reduce confectioners' sugar in half
  Add 1 tablespoon crème de menthe liqueur

MOCHA CHIP CREAM
  ½ teaspoon instant coffee

ORANGE LIQUEUR CHIP CREAM
  Omit vanilla and reduce confectioners' sugar in half
  Add 1 tablespoon orange liqueur

RUM CHIP CREAM
  Omit vanilla
  Add ½ teaspoon rum extract

Chocolate Whipped Cream

Makes about 1½ cups

⅔ cup semisweet chocolate
　chips
2 tablespoons light corn syrup

2 tablespoons water
1 cup whipping cream
1 teaspoon vanilla

Melt chocolate chips with corn syrup and water in a small heavy saucepan over low heat, stirring until smooth. Remove from heat; cool. Beat whipping cream and vanilla in a chilled small bowl with chilled beaters until stiff. Gently fold cooled chocolate mixture into whipped cream. Spread filling between cooled cake layers.

The Allegretti style of garnishing (also known as shadow garnishing) can easily dress up a layer or tube cake. Melt ⅓ cup semisweet chocolate chips and 1½ tablespoons butter in top of a double boiler over simmering water, stirring until smooth. Drizzle chocolate on the top outer edge of a white or light-colored frosted cake, allowing the chocolate to drip down the sides of the cake.

Chocolate Chip Candy

Chocolate chips are ideal for candy making since it is not necessary to temper them. In this chapter you will find a truly innovative array of candies to satisfy every taste, all made with chips used in imaginative ways. There are opulent fudges, simple chocolate nut clusters, and crunchy toffees. You will find recipes for bonbons dipped into melted chips, and when calories are of no consequence, there are melt-in-the-mouth sinfully rich truffles, filled with melted and whipped chocolate chips. Some candies are filled or crusted with fruit or nuts; others are pure chocolate delights. The recipes are designed to make the Willy Wonkas of the world ecstatic.

Candies

Chocolate Cream Cheese Fudge

Makes about 1 pound

1 cup semisweet chocolate chips	*1 teaspoon vanilla*
1 8-ounce package cream	*Dash of salt*
cheese, softened	*1 cup nuts, chopped*

Line an 8-inch square pan with aluminum foil. Melt chocolate chips in top of a double boiler over simmering water, stirring until smooth. Remove from heat. Beat cream cheese in a small mixing bowl on medium speed until light and fluffy. Blend in melted chocolate chips, mixing well. Add vanilla and salt. Stir in chopped nuts with a spoon. Spread mixture in prepared pan. Chill until firm, approximately 2 hours. Remove from pan; peel foil from fudge. Cut into 1-inch squares. Store fudge in refrigerator.

Crispy Chocolate Fudge

Makes 64 pieces

1 cup semisweet chocolate chips	*1½ teaspoons vanilla*
¼ cup butter	*1 cup confectioners' sugar,*
¼ cup light corn syrup	*sifted*
	3 cups crispy rice cereal

Grease an 8-inch square pan; set aside. Melt chocolate chips and butter in a 3-quart heavy saucepan over low heat, stirring until smooth. Remove from heat; stir in corn syrup and vanilla. Add sifted confectioners' sugar, blending well. Stir in rice cereal. Spread mixture in prepared pan. Cover and chill until firm, about 2 hours. Cut candy into 1-inch squares.

Variation: For Crispy Chocolate Cherry Fudge, add ½ cup maraschino cherries, chopped and well drained.

Peanut Butter Fudge

Makes 81 pieces

2 cups granulated sugar	*1 cup peanut butter*
⅔ cup milk	*1 cup semisweet chocolate chips*
1 cup marshmallow crème	*1 teaspoon vanilla*

Line a 9-inch square pan with aluminum foil; grease foil. Butter bottom and sides of a 2-quart heavy saucepan. Combine sugar and milk in prepared saucepan. Cook, stirring constantly, until sugar dissolves and mixture boils. Continue cooking until mixture reaches 234°F (soft-ball stage) on a candy thermometer. Remove from heat, and quickly stir in marshmallow crème, peanut butter, chocolate chips, and vanilla; blend well. Pour fudge into prepared pan. Score into 1-inch squares. When firm, remove fudge from pan; peel off foil. Cut into 1-inch pieces.

Candy should be made on a cool, clear day; hot, humid weather can cause candy to be sticky.

Boiled Candy

Makes about 3½ dozen

2½ cups oatmeal	*½ cup butter*
½ cup flaked coconut	*½ cup semisweet chocolate*
½ cup nuts, chopped	*chips*
2 cups granulated sugar	*1 teaspoon vanilla*
½ cup milk	*2 tablespoons peanut butter*

Cover two cookie sheets with wax paper. Combine oatmeal, coconut, and chopped nuts in a large bowl; set aside. Bring sugar, milk, and butter to a full boil in a 2-quart heavy saucepan. Stir in chocolate chips and vanilla; blend until chocolate is melted. Remove from heat, and stir in peanut butter. Pour mixture over dry ingredients in bowl; quickly stir together. Drop candy by teaspoonfuls onto prepared cookie sheets. Cool to set.

Chocolate Peanut Butter Raisin Clusters

Makes about 5 dozen

2 cups semisweet chocolate
  chips

1 cup peanut butter
2½ cups raisins

Cover two cookie sheets with wax paper. Melt chocolate chips with peanut butter in top of a double boiler over simmering water. Remove from heat; stir in raisins. Drop candy by teaspoonfuls onto prepared cookie sheets. Chill until firm, about 1 hour.

Dark Chocolate Cashew Clusters

Makes about 4 dozen

2 cups semisweet chocolate
  chips

1 1-ounce square unsweetened
  chocolate
2 cups cashew nuts

Cover two cookie sheets with wax paper. Melt chocolates in top of a double boiler over simmering water, stirring until smooth. Remove from heat; stir in cashew nuts. Drop by teaspoonfuls onto prepared cookie sheets. Chill until set. Store candy in a tightly covered container in refrigerator.

Chocolate Bark

Makes about 1 pound

2 cups semisweet chocolate
   chips
1 cup sweetened condensed
   milk

1 cup raisins
1 cup nuts, chopped coarse
1 teaspoon vanilla

Line a 15½ × 10½ × 1-inch jelly roll pan with aluminum foil; grease foil. Melt chocolate chips in top of a double boiler over simmering water, stirring until smooth. Stir in sweetened condensed milk, blending well. Remove from heat; stir in raisins, chopped nuts, and vanilla. Pour mixture into prepared pan. Spread candy over pan with a knife. Chill until firm, about 2 hours. When candy is firm, break it into chunks. Store candy in refrigerator.

Note: Raisins may be soaked in 2 tablespoons dark rum overnight if desired.

Rocky Road

Makes about 9 dozen

5½ cups mini marshmallows
1⅔ cups unsalted peanuts
2 cups semisweet chocolate
   chips

1 1-ounce square unsweetened
   chocolate
2 tablespoons butter
1 14-ounce can sweetened
   condensed milk

Line a 13 × 9 × 2-inch pan with aluminum foil. Mix together mini marshmallows and peanuts in a large bowl; set aside. Melt chocolates and butter with sweetened condensed milk in a 2-quart heavy saucepan over low heat, stirring until smooth. Pour melted chocolate mixture over ingredients in bowl; stir to coat evenly. Spread candy in prepared pan. Chill for 2 hours, or until set. Remove from pan; peel foil from candy. Cut into 1-inch squares with a wet knife. Store candy in refrigerator.

Most candy will keep for several weeks if put into an airtight container and stored in a cool, dry place. Candies that should be refrigerated are designated.

Chocolate-Topped Peanut Butter Candy

Makes 64 pieces

½ cut butter
⅔ cup graham cracker crumbs
2 cups confectioners' sugar

¾ cup peanut butter
¾ cup semisweet chocolate chips

Line an 8-inch square pan with aluminum foil. Melt butter in a small saucepan over low heat; remove from heat. Mix together graham cracker crumbs, confectioners' sugar, and peanut butter in a small mixing bowl on low speed. Add melted butter, blending well. Press mixture into prepared pan. Melt chocolate chips in top of a double boiler over simmering water, stirring until smooth. Spread melted chocolate chips over peanut butter mixture. Chill for 30 minutes to set chocolate. Remove candy from refrigerator, and leave at room temperature for at least 1 hour. Remove from pan; peel foil from candy. Cut into 1-inch squares.

Chocolate-Topped Goody Bars

Makes about 3 dozen

¼ cup butter
1 10-ounce package mini
  marshmallows

7 cups crispy rice cereal
1 cup peanuts, chopped coarse

TOPPING
½ cups semisweet chocolate
  chips
3 tablespoons butter

Grease a cookie sheet; set aside. Melt butter and marshmallows in a 4-quart heavy saucepan over low heat, stirring frequently, until smooth. Remove saucepan from heat; stir in rice cereal and chopped peanuts until well coated. Spoon mixture onto prepared cookie sheet; cool for 5 minutes. With buttered hands, press mixture into a 12 × 9-inch rectangle. Cool until firm.

For topping melt chocolate chips with butter in a small saucepan over low heat, stirring until smooth. Remove from heat. Drizzle chocolate mixture with a spoon over rectangle. Cool until chocolate is set. Cut into bars. Eat within 2 days.

Heavenly Sweets

Makes about 4 dozen

1 cup semisweet chocolate chips
2 tablespoons butter
1 egg, beaten
1 cup confectioners' sugar,
  sifted

2 cups mini marshmallows
1 cup nuts, chopped
1 cup flaked coconut

Cover a cookie sheet with wax paper; set aside. Melt chocolate chips and butter in top of a double boiler over simmering water, stirring until smooth. Remove from heat; blend in beaten egg. Add sifted confectioners' sugar and marshmallows, blending until marshmallows are melted. Stir in chopped nuts. Cool mixture until it can be handled. Shape into 1-inch balls; roll in coconut. Place candy on prepared cookie sheet, and chill until set, about 2 hours. Store in an airtight container in refrigerator.

Chocolate-Nut Bonbons

Makes 4½ dozen

⅔ cup brown sugar, packed
    firm
¼ cup light corn syrup
2 tablespoons butter

2 tablespoons whipping cream
1½ cups nuts, chopped fine
½ teaspoon rum extract

CHOCOLATE COATING
⅓ cup semisweet chocolate
    chips
2 1-ounce squares unsweetened
    chocolate

2 tablespoons butter
2 tablespoons light corn syrup

Combine brown sugar, corn syrup, butter, and whipping cream in a 2-quart heavy saucepan over medium heat. Cook, stirring constantly, until mixture comes to a boil; boil for 2 minutes. Stir in chopped nuts. Cook, stirring constantly, for 1 minute longer. Remove from heat; stir in rum extract. Pour mixture into a bowl. Cool for 15 minutes. Then chill mixture for about 1 hour, or until completely cool.

Cover a cookie sheet with wax paper. Shape nut mixture into ¾-inch balls. Place candy on prepared cookie sheet; set aside.

For chocolate coating, melt chocolates and butter with corn syrup in top of a double boiler over simmering water, stirring until smooth. Remove from heat; keep double boiler over water. Using a fork, dip each ball into chocolate, allowing excess chocolate to drip back into pan. (If coating becomes too thick, reheat until it is the correct consistency.) Chill for about 45 minutes to set chocolate. Store candy in refrigerator. Eat within 2 weeks.

Peanut Butter Bonbons

Makes about 4 dozen

1 tablespoon butter
2 tablespoons evaporated milk
½ teaspoon vanilla
Dash of salt

2 cups confectioners' sugar, sifted
1 cup creamy peanut butter
1 tablespoon dark corn syrup
1 cup semisweet chocolate chips

Cover a cookie sheet with wax paper; set aside. Melt butter in a 3-quart heavy saucepan over low heat. Stir in evaporated milk, vanilla, and salt; remove from heat. Gradually add 1½ cups sifted confectioners' sugar, stirring until mixture is thick and smooth. Add peanut butter and corn syrup; blend well. Turn mixture onto a surface dusted with remaining ½ cup confectioners' sugar. Knead mixture until it becomes thick and dough-like. Form slightly rounded teaspoonfuls of the mixture into balls. Melt chocolate chips in top of a double boiler over simmering water, stirring until smooth. Remove from heat; keep double boiler over water. Using a toothpick, dip each ball into melted chocolate chips just until half-coated. Place candy on prepared cookie sheet. Chill until firm. Store candy in refrigerator.

Chocolate Walnut Creams

Makes about 4 dozen

1⅓ cups semisweet chocolate chips
1 cup confectioners' sugar
1 tablespoon dark rum

1 egg, at room temperature and beaten
2 cups walnuts, chopped fine
Foil candy cups

Melt chocolate chips in top of a double boiler over simmering water, stirring until smooth. Remove from heat, and stir in confectioners' sugar, rum, and beaten egg; beat until well blended. Cool for 10 minutes; then place mixture in refrigerator until firm enough to shape, about 2 hours.

Place a sheet of wax paper on a cookie sheet. Spread chopped walnuts on another sheet of wax paper. Shape chilled chocolate mixture into ½-inch balls; roll in walnuts. Place candy on prepared cookie sheet. Let stand for 1 hour. Put finished candies in foil candy cups.

Chocolate Truffles

Makes about 3 dozen

1 cup whipping cream
⅔ cup granulated sugar
¾ cup butter

2 cups mini chocolate chips
2 teaspoons vanilla
1½ cups nuts, chopped fine

Combine cream, sugar, and butter in a 2-quart heavy saucepan over medium heat; bring to boil. Immediately remove from heat, and stir in mini chocolate chips, blending until melted. Add vanilla. Pour mixture into a bowl, and stir occasionally until cool. Cover bowl; chill overnight.

Working quickly to prevent melting, shape chilled mixture into ½-inch balls. Roll truffles in chopped nuts. Store in refrigerator; serve cold.

Chocolate Nut Truffles

Makes about 2 dozen

1⅓ cups semisweet chocolate
    chips
¾ cup nuts, chopped fine
1 cup confectioners' sugar

2 tablespoons light cream
1 teaspoon vanilla

Melt chocolate chips in top of a double boiler over simmering water, stirring until smooth. Add chopped nuts, confectioners' sugar, light cream, and vanilla; stir until well blended. Remove from heat. Cool for 20 minutes, or until mixture is stiff enough to handle. With buttered hands, shape cooled mixture into ¾-inch balls. Place truffles on a jelly roll pan. Chill for 30 minutes, or until firm. Store truffles in refrigerator.

Truffles should be stored in a refrigerator. Once removed, they should be eaten within 30 minutes or they will become too soft. Truffles will keep for up to 1 week.

Coffee Liqueur Truffles

Makes about 3 dozen

2 cups semisweet chocolate   ⅓ cup coffee liqueur
   chips   ⅔ cup butter, cut into pieces
4 egg yolks   1½ cups pecans, chopped fine

Melt chocolate chips in top of a double boiler over simmering water, stirring until smooth. Remove top of boiler from heat; cool to room temperature. Add egg yolks, one at a time, stirring constantly until mixture is thoroughly blended. Stir in coffee liqueur, and return top of double boiler to simmering water. Cook, stirring constantly, for 2 to 3 minutes. Pour mixture into a small mixing bowl. Beat in butter, one piece at a time on medium speed. Continue to beat until mixture is fluffy. Cover bowl, and chill for 5 hours or overnight.

Shape chilled mixture into ¾-inch balls; roll in chopped pecans. Store truffles in refrigerator until ready to serve.

Note: Coffee Liqueur Truffles freeze well if placed in an airtight container with wax paper between layers of candy.

Variations: Any of the following combinations may be substituted for the coffee liqueur and chopped pecans:

AMARETTO TRUFFLES
⅓ *cup amaretto liqueur*
1½ *cups blanched almonds, chopped fine*

CRÈME DE MENTHE TRUFFLES
⅓ *cup creme de menthe liqueur*
¼ *cup unsweetened cocoa, sifted with*
2 *tablespoons sugar*

ORANGE LIQUEUR TRUFFLES
⅓ *cup orange liqueur*
1½ *cups hazelnuts, chopped fine*

RASPBERRY LIQUEUR TRUFFLES
⅓ *cup raspberry liqueur*
1½ *cups walnuts, chopped fine*

Pecan Turtles

Makes about 3 dozen

½ *cup quartered pecans (pecan*   ⅔ *cup pecans, chopped*
 halves broken in half   ⅔ *cup semisweet chocolate*
 lengthwise)   *chips*
30 *vanilla caramels*

Cover a cookie sheet with wax paper. Arrange three pecan quarters on prepared cookie sheet to represent a turtle's head and front legs; repeat procedure until all the quarters are used.

Melt caramels in top of a double boiler over simmering water, stirring until smooth. Stir in chopped pecans. Drop caramel mixture by teaspoonfuls onto arranged pecan quarters to form bodies. (Make sure that the tips of the pecan quarters extend from the caramel.) Cool.

Melt chocolate chips in top of a double boiler over simmering water, stirring until smooth. Frost caramel bodies with melted chocolate chips. Allow chocolate to set. Store in an airtight container with wax paper between layers of turtles.

Note: Do not chill Pecan Turtles; the caramel will "sweat."

Another way to shape Pecan Turtles is to wait until the melted caramel mixture is cool enough to handle; then, with buttered hands, shape into balls and insert three pecan quarters. Press caramel bodies to cookie sheet to flatten slightly.

Chocolate Caramel Apples

Makes 6

6 medium apples	¼ cup semisweet chocolate
6 wooden skewers	chips
½ cup nuts, chopped	50 vanilla caramels
	2 tablespoons hot water

Wash and dry apples; insert wooden skewer into each. Cover a cookie sheet with wax paper. Place chopped nuts, divided into six equal mounds, on prepared cookie sheet.

Melt chocolate chips and caramels with hot water in top of a double boiler over simmering water, stirring until smooth. Remove from heat; keep double boiler over water. Quickly spread mixture over apples with a knife. Roll bottom half of each apple in a mound of chopped nuts. Cool to set.

Frozen Banana Pops

Makes 6

3 bananas	2 cups semisweet chocolate
6 wooden skewers	chips
	½ cup hot water

Peel bananas, and cut in halves crosswise; insert a wooden skewer into each half. Place bananas on a cookie sheet, and freeze for 1 hour.

Cut six aluminum foil squares; set aside. Melt chocolate chips in hot water in top of a double boiler over simmering water, stirring until smooth. Dip frozen banana halves into melted chocolate mixture, covering completely; allow excess chocolate to drip back into double boiler. When chocolate is set, wrap in foil squares, and return banana pops to freezer until ready to serve.

Note: After banana halves have been dipped in chocolate, they may be rolled in 1 cup chopped nuts or flaked coconut if desired.

Chocolate Cherry Cordials

Makes 2 dozen

3 tablespoon kirsch
1 tablespoon grenadine syrup
1 cup mini chocolate chips

24 1-inch foil candy cases
1 clean ¼-inch paintbrush
24 candied or maraschino
    cherries

Combine kirsch and grenadine syrup in a small bowl; chill.

Melt chocolate chips in top of a double boiler over simmering water, stirring until smooth; keep warm. Spoon a small amount of melted chocolate into a foil candy case, and paint onto bottom and sides. Repeat procedure with remaining candy cases. Place candy cases on a jelly roll pan, and chill for 5 minutes to set chocolate. When chocolate is set, place a cherry in each candy case. Drizzle enough kirsch mixture into each candy case to fill halfway. Spoon remaining chocolate over each cherry to fill candy case. Chill for 5 minutes, or until chocolate is set. Store in an airtight container. Let candy stand for at least 24 hours before serving.

Variation: For Mini Pots of Cream, omit kirsch mixture and cherries. Instead, fill chocolate-coated candy cases with sweetened whipped cream. Mini Pots of Cream are excellent eaten as is or dropped into coffee or hot chocolate.

Chocolate-Covered Pretzels

Makes about 3 dozen

1 cup semisweet chocolate chips   1½ teaspoon water
2 tablespoons butter   1 9-ounce package mini
2 tablespoons light corn syrup   pretzels or pretzel sticks

Place a wire rack over a cookie sheet; set aside. Melt chocolate chips and butter with corn syrup and water in top of a double boiler over simmering water, stirring until smooth. Remove from heat; keep double boiler over water. Using a fork, dip pretzels into melted chocolate mixture to coat thoroughly. Place pretzels on wire rack. Refrigerate for about 10 minutes, or until chocolate coating is set. Remove from refrigerator, and let pretzels stand at room temperature for 1 hour, or until chocolate is dry.

Chocolate Caramels

Makes 81 pieces

2 cups granulated sugar   2 cups whipping cream
1 cup light corn syrup   ½ cup butter, cut into pieces
⅓ semisweet chocolate chips   1 teaspoon vanilla

Line a 9-inch square pan with aluminum foil; grease foil. Lightly oil a 3-quart heavy saucepan. Combine sugar and corn syrup in prepared saucepan; cook over medium-low heat, stirring constantly, until the sugar is completely dissolved. Add chocolate chips, stirring until melted. Bring mixture to a boil. Meanwhile, in a saucepan over low heat, heat whipping cream to lukewarm. Place a candy thermometer in the chocolate mixture, and continue to cook until mixture reaches 250°F (hard-ball stage). Slowly pour warmed cream into chocolate mixture; *the mixture should never stop boiling.* Cook, stirring constantly, until temperature again reaches 250°F. Add butter, one piece at a time, again making sure that the mixture never stops boiling. Cook until thermometer once more reaches 250°F. Remove saucepan from heat; stir in vanilla. Pour mixture in a steady stream into prepared pan. (Do not scrape saucepan.) Cool for 2 hours; then chill until caramel is firm, about 1-2 hours. Remove from pan; peel foil from caramel. Cut into 1-inch squares. Wrap caramels individually in wax paper. Store in an airtight container in refrigerator.

Note: For softer caramels, remove from refrigerator 30 minutes before serving.

When cooking candy, use a heavy saucepan; this will prevent burning. To help prevent candy from boiling over, lightly oil the inside of the saucepan before starting. Also, it is a good idea to use a saucepan that will hold about four times the volume of the candy mixture to ensure that it will not boil over.

Raisin Caramels

Makes about 5 dozen

1 cup raisins
¾ cup butter

1 cup brown sugar, packed
firm
1 cup semisweet chocolate chips

Line an 8-inch square pan with aluminum foil; grease foil. Sprinkle raisins over bottom of prepared pan; set aside. Combine butter and brown sugar in a 2-quart heavy saucepan over medium heat. Cook, stirring constantly, until mixture reaches 254°F (hard-ball stage) on a candy thermometer. Pour mixture over raisins in pan. Sprinkle with chocolate chips; let stand for 5 minutes. Using a knife, frost caramel with chocolate chips. Cool for 30 minutes; then chill until chocolate is firm, about 1 hour. Remove from pan; peel foil from caramels. Cut caramels into 1-inch squares; wrap individually in wax paper. Store in an airtight container in refrigerator.

Chocolate Peanut Brittle

Makes 2 pounds

2 cups granulated sugar
1 cup light corn syrup
½ cup water
2 tablespoons butter

2 cups peanuts
1 cup semisweet chocolate chips
1½ teaspoons vanilla

Generously grease a large cookie sheet; set aside. Combine sugar, corn syrup, and water in a 3-quart heavy saucepan over medium-low heat. Bring mixture to a boil, stirring constantly, until sugar is dissolved. Cover pan, and cook for 2 minutes. Uncover pan, and cook *without* stirring until mixture reaches 252°F (hard-ball stage) on a candy thermometer. Stir in butter and peanuts. Continue to cook, stirring constantly, until mixture reaches 300°F (hard-crack stage). Remove from heat; quickly stir in chocolate chips and vanilla, blending until chocolate is melted. Pour onto prepared cookie sheet. Using two forks and starting from center, stretch and pull candy until it covers the cookie sheet. Cool candy completely. Break candy into pieces.

Chocolate Walnut Butter Toffee

Makes about 2 pounds

2¼ cups granulated sugar
1¼ cups butter
½ cup water
¼ teaspoon salt

2 cups walnuts, chopped
1 cup semisweet chocolate chips
½ cup walnuts, chopped

Line a 15½ × 10½ × 1-inch jelly roll pan with aluminum foil; grease foil. Combine sugar, butter, water, and salt in a 3-quart heavy saucepan over medium heat. Cook, stirring constantly with a wooden spoon, until mixture reaches 325°F on a candy thermometer. Stir in 2 cups chopped walnuts. Pour mixture into prepared pan; spread evenly. Cool.

Melt chocolate chips in top of a double boiler over simmering water, stirring until smooth. Spread cooled toffee with melted chocolate; sprinkle with ½ cup chopped walnuts. Cool to set chocolate. Remove from pan; peel foil from toffee. Break into pieces.

Variations: For a different flavor add any one of the following along with the 2 cups chopped walnuts:

1½ teaspoons brandy extract   *1½ teaspoons rum extract*
2 teaspoons maple extract   *2 teaspoons vanilla extract*
½ teaspoon orange extract

Orange Chocolate Toffee

Makes about 1 pound

1 cup granulated sugar   *1 cup semisweet chocolate chips*
1 cup butter   *½ cup pecans, chopped coarse*
3 tablespoons water   *2 tablespoons grated orange*
1 teaspoon vanilla   *peel*

Generously grease a large cookie sheet. Combine sugar, butter, water, and vanilla in a 2-quart heavy saucepan over medium heat. Bring mixture to a boil, stirring frequently, until sugar is dissolved. Continue cooking, stirring constantly, for about 30 minutes, or until mixture reaches 310°F (hard-crack stage) on a candy thermometer. Pour toffee mixture onto prepared cookie sheet.

Melt chocolate chips in top of a double boiler over simmering water, stirring until smooth. Spread melted chocolate over toffee; sprinkle with chopped pecans and orange peel. Place cookie sheet on a wire rack; cool candy completely, about 1 hour. When candy is cool, break into pieces. Store in an airtight container. Orange Chocolate Toffee will keep for up to 2 weeks.

Brandy Pecan Butter Creams

Makes about 3 pounds

½ cup pecans, chopped fine
3 tablespoons brandy
4½ cups granulated sugar
½ cup light corn syrup

1 cup water
½ cup butter, cut into ½-inch
*   pieces*
3⅓ cups semisweet chocolate
*   chips*

In small bowl, soak chopped pecans in brandy for at least 2 hours or overnight, if possible.

Combine sugar, corn syrup, and water in a 4-quart heavy pan over medium heat; bring to a boil. Cook, stirring constantly, until syrup mixture reaches 220°F on a candy thermometer. Add butter, one piece at a time, stirring until melted. Cover pan, and cook for 2 minutes. Uncover pan, and continue to cook until mixture reaches 242°F (soft-ball stage). Pour mixture onto a marble slab or large platter; cool to 98°F, about 15 to 20 minutes. Fold edges to center with a wide spatula until candy changes to a creamy color, approximately 30 minutes. With buttered hands, mix brandy-soaked pecans into candy; knead until smooth. Divide into six equal parts; roll each part into a 1-inch-wide log on a sheet of wax paper. Wrap logs in wax paper, and store overnight at room temperature.

Cover two cookie sheets with wax paper. Remove wax paper from logs, and cut into ¾-inch pieces; roll each piece into a ball. Melt chocolate chips in top of a double boiler over simmering water, stirring until smooth. Keep melted chocolate warm. Using a fork, dip each ball into chocolate, coating completely. Set candy on prepared cookie sheets. Allow chocolate to set.

Note: Shaped like eggs, Brandy Pecan Butter Creams make an excellent Easter gift for that special kid.

Variations: For a change, try using any one of the following instead of pecans and brandy:

CHERRY BUTTER CREAMS
⅓ cup candied cherries, well drained and chopped fine.

COCONUT BUTTER CREAMS
½ cup flaked coconut
½ teaspoon almond extract

MAPLE WALNUT BUTTER CREAMS
½ cup walnuts, chopped fine
1½ teaspoons maple extract

ORANGE ALMOND BUTTER CREAMS
½ cup blanched almonds, chopped fine
½ to ¾ teaspoon orange extract

RUM HAZELNUT BUTTER CREAMS
½ cup hazelnuts, chopped fine
3 tablespoons dark rum

When using a candy thermometer, do not allow it to touch the bottom or sides of pan, or the temperature reading will not be accurate.

Orange Butter Crunch Popcorn

Makes about 1½ pounds

8 cups popped popcorn,
  unsalted
1 cup peanuts
Grated peel of 1 orange
1 cup plus 2 tablespoons
  granulated sugar

½ cup plus 2 tablespoons
  butter
¼ cup orange juice
½ cup mini chocolate chips

Grease a 15½ × 10½ × 1-inch jelly roll pan; set aside. Grease a large bowl. Toss together popcorn, peanuts, and orange peel in prepared bowl. Combine sugar, butter, and orange juice in a 3-quart heavy saucepan over medium heat. Cook, stirring constantly, until mixture reaches 325°F on a candy thermometer. Pour over popcorn mixture, and toss to coat. Spread candy on prepared jelly roll pan; sprinkle with mini chocolate chips. Cool completely. Break candy into pieces.

Cookies Featuring Chips

Since the introduction of the toll house cookie the chocolate chip cookie craze shows little sign of calming. As the following chapter can attest, the search for the perfect chocolate chip cookie does not have to end with Mrs. Wakefield's creation. Thousands of cookie recipes are just begging to be perfected by having chocolate chips incorporated into them in a new way. The versatile chocolate chip is a delicious addition to practically any type of cookie, be it bar, drop, molded, or refrigerator. Some of the following recipes are old standards, but many were created by adding chips to family favorites, making them even more enjoyable by the introduction of chocolate. So whether a cookie is studded with chocolate chips, intersticed with a chocolate chip filling, or frosted with a chocolate chip glaze, it will be many bites ahead of the rest!

COOKIES

BAR COOKIE SIZE
AND NUMBER TABLE

The following table is a guide to help determine the number and approximate size of bar cookies.

Size of Pan	Number of Cuts Lengthwise/Crosswise	Approximate Size of Bar	Number of Bars
9-inch square	2/5	3 × 1½-inch	18
	3/5	2¼ × 1½-inch	24
	5/5	1½ × 1½-inch	36
13 × 9 × 2-inch oblong	2/7	3 × 1⅝-inch	24
	5/5	1½ × 2⅛-inch	36
	7/5	1⅛ × 2⅛-inch	48
15½ × 10½ × 1-inch jelly roll	3/8	2⅝ × 1¾-inch	36
	3/11	2⅝ × 1¼-inch	48
	3/14	2⅝ × 1-inch	60
	7/8	1¼ × 1¾-inch	72

Marshmallow Brownies

Makes 1½ dozen

1 cup semisweet chocolate chips
½ cup butter
1½ cups mini marshmallows
2 eggs

1 teaspoon vanilla
½ cup all-purpose flour
¼ teaspoon baking powder
½ cup nuts, chopped

CHOCOLATE MARSHMALLOW FROSTING

¼ cup semisweet chocolate
  chips
½ cup mini marshmallows
2 tablespoons butter

1 cup confectioners' sugar,
  sifted
2 teaspoons milk

Melt chocolate chips, butter, and marshmallows in a 2-quart heavy saucepan over low heat, stirring until smooth. Remove from heat; cool for 10 minutes.

Grease a 9-inch square pan; set aside. Preheat oven to 350°F. Beat eggs, one at a time, into melted chocolate mixture. Add vanilla. Blend in flour and baking powder, mixing well. Stir in chopped nuts. Spread batter in prepared pan. Bake for 15 to 20 minutes. Cool completely.

For chocolate marshmallow frosting, melt chocolate chips, marshmallows, and butter in a small heavy saucepan over low heat, stirring until smooth. Remove from heat. Add sifted confectioners' sugar and milk; beat until smooth. Quickly spread frosting over cooled brownies. Cool to set frosting.

Rum Brownies

Makes 1½ dozen

⅓ cup butter
½ cup granulated sugar
2 tablespoons water
1 cup semisweet chocolate chips
1 teaspoon vanilla

2 eggs
¾ cup all-purpose flour
¼ teaspoon baking powder
½ cup nuts, chopped
¼ cup dark rum

FROSTING

3 tablespoons butter, softened
1½ cups confectioners' sugar
¼ teaspoon vanilla
2 to 3 teaspoons milk

¼ cup semisweet chocolate
  chips
1½ tablespoons butter

Combine butter, granulated sugar, and water in a 2-quart heavy saucepan over medium heat. Cook, stirring constantly, until mixture boils. Remove from heat; add chocolate chips, stirring until melted. Add vanilla. Cool for 10 minutes.

Grease a 9-inch square baking pan. Preheat oven to 350°F. Beat eggs, one at a time, into melted chocolate mixture. Add flour and baking powder, blending well. Stir in chopped nuts. Spread batter in prepared pan. Bake for 20 to 30 minutes, or until a toothpick inserted in center comes out clean. Remove from oven; drizzle rum over top of brownies. Cool completely.

For frosting, beat together 3 tablespoons softened butter, confectioners' sugar, vanilla, and milk in a small mixing bowl on medium speed until smooth. Frost cooled brownies. Melt chocolate chips and 1½ tablespoons butter in a measuring cup set in simmering water, stirring until smooth. Drizzle melted chocolate mixture over frosting with a spoon. Allow frosting to set. Cut into bars.

Note: For teetotalers, omit rum and frosting. Instead, immediately upon removing brownies from oven, sprinkle with an additional 1 cup semisweet chocolate chips; let stand for 5 minutes. Frost brownies with chocolate chips; sprinkle with ½ cup crispy rice cereal.

Be sure to spread bar cookie dough evenly in pan. Completely cool bar cookies before frosting, unless otherwise stated. Bar cookies may be kept in the pan they are baked in if tightly covered.

Chocolate Chip Pan Bars

Makes 4 dozen

½ cup butter, softened
1½ cups brown sugar, packed
   firm
3 eggs
1½ teaspoon vanilla

2½ cups all-purpose flour,
   sifted
1 cup nuts, chopped coarse
1½ cups semisweet chocolate
   chips

Grease a 15½ × 10½ × 1-inch jelly roll pan; set aside. Preheat oven to 350°F. Cream butter and brown sugar in a large mixing bowl on medium speed until fluffy. Add eggs, one at a time, blending well after each addition. Add vanilla. Lower speed, and add sifted flour, blending well. Stir in chopped nuts and chocolate chips with a spoon. Spread dough in prepared pan. Bake for 30 to 35 minutes. Cool. Cut into bars.

Variation: For Fruit and Chip Pan Bars, omit nuts; instead, add ½ cup each raisins, chopped dates, and drained and chopped maraschino cherries.

Candy Bars

Makes 4 dozen

BASE

2 cups all-purpose flour	2 tablespoons milk
¾ cup confectioners' sugar	1½ teaspoons vanilla
¾ cup butter, softened	

FILLING

28 vanilla caramels	¾ cup confectioners' sugar,
¼ cup milk	sifted
¼ cup butter	1 cup nuts, chopped fine

GLAZE

2 cups semisweet chocolate chips	½ cup butter

Preheat oven to 325°F. For base, toss together flour and confectioners' sugar in a bowl. Cut in butter with a pastry blender or two knives used scissor-fashion until mixture resembles coarse crumbs. Add milk and vanilla, blending until mixture holds together. Press mixture onto the bottom of an ungreased 15½ × 10½ × 1-inch jelly roll pan. Bake for 15 to 20 minutes, or until golden.

Meanwhile, for filling, melt caramels, milk, and butter in a heavy saucepan over medium-low heat, stirring until smooth. Remove from heat; stir in sifted confectioners' sugar and chopped nuts. Immediately upon removing base from oven, spread it with filling.

For glaze, melt chocolate chips and butter in top of a double boiler over simmering water, stirring until smooth. Remove from heat. Carefully spread glaze over filling. Cool completely. Cut into bars.

Cinnamon Streusel Bars

Makes 4 dozen

STREUSEL

2½ cups all-purpose flour
½ cup brown sugar, packed firm
¼ teaspoon baking powder

1 teaspoon cinnamon
¾ cup butter, softened

BASE

2 cups all-purpose flour
2 cups oatmeal
1 cup brown sugar, packed firm
½ teaspoon baking powder

1 cup butter, softened
1 cup nuts, chopped coarse
2 cups semisweet chocolate chips

For streusel, stir together flour, brown sugar, baking powder, and cinnamon in a large bowl. Cut in butter with a pastry blender or two knives used scissor-fashion until mixture resembles coarse crumbs. Set aside.

Preheat oven to 350°F. For base, stir together flour, oatmeal, brown sugar, and baking powder in a large bowl. Cut in butter with a pastry blender or two knives used scissor-fashion until mixture resembles crumbs. Press dough into an ungreased 15½ × 10½ × 1-inch jelly roll pan. Bake for 5 minutes. Immediately upon removing base from oven, sprinkle with chopped nuts and chocolate chips. Crumble streusel on top, and lightly press in. Return to oven, and bake for 35 minutes longer, or until golden. Cool. Cut into bars.

Coffee Pecan Chip Bars

Makes 1½ dozen

½ cup butter, softened
¾ cup brown sugar, packed
*   firm*
1 egg
1 tablespoon instant coffee
½ teaspoon vanilla

1¼ cups all-purpose flour
½ teaspoon baking soda
¾ cup pecans, chopped
1 cup semisweet chocolate chips

COFFEE ICING
2 tablespoons butter
1 tablespoon milk
1 teaspoon instant coffee

1⅓ cups confectioners' sugar,
*   sifted*

Grease a 9-inch square pan; set aside. Preheat oven to 375°F. Cream butter and brown sugar in a mixing bowl on medium speed until fluffy. Beat in egg, instant coffee, and vanilla. Lower speed, and add flour and baking soda; blend well. Stir in chopped pecans and chocolate chips with a spoon. Spread dough in prepared pan. Bake for 25 to 30 minutes. Cool completely.

For coffee icing, melt butter in a saucepan over low heat. Remove from heat; stir in milk and instant coffee. Add sifted confectioners' sugar, beating until smooth. (If icing is too thick, add a drop or two of milk.) Frost cooled cookies with icing; allow to set. Cut into bars.

Banana Chip Bars

Makes 4 dozen

¾ cup butter, softened
⅔ cup granulated sugar
⅔ cup brown sugar, packed
   firm
1 egg
1 teaspoon vanilla

1 cup mashed bananas
2 cups all-purpose flour
2 teaspoons baking powder
1 cup semisweet chocolate chips
1 cup nuts, chopped

Grease a 15½ × 10½ × 1-inch jelly roll pan; set aside. Preheat oven to 350°F. Cream butter and sugars in a mixing bowl on medium speed until fluffy. Beat in egg and vanilla. Add mashed bananas, blending well. Lower speed, and add flour and baking powder. Stir in chocolate chips with a spoon. Spread dough in prepared pan; sprinkle with chopped nuts. Bake for 25 minutes, or until golden. Cool. Cut into bars.

Coconut Chip Layer Bars

Makes 2 dozen

BASE
½ cup butter, softened
1½ cups brown sugar, packed
   firm

1 cup all-purpose flour

FILLING
2 eggs
½ cup whipping cream
1 teaspoon vanilla
⅓ cup all-purpose flour

1 teaspoon baking powder
1½ cups flaked coconut
⅓ cup mini chocolate chips

Grease a 9-inch square pan; set aside. Preheat oven to 350°F. For base, cream butter and brown sugar in a small mixing bowl on medium speed until fluffy. Lower speed, and add flour. Press mixture into the bottom of prepared pan. Bake for 20 to 25 minutes, or until golden.

Meanwhile, for filling, beat eggs in a small mixing bowl on medium speed until lemon-colored. Blend in cream and vanilla. Lower speed, and add flour and baking powder. Stir in coconut with a spoon. Immediately upon removing base from oven, pour filling over it, and sprinkle with mini chocolate chips. Return to oven, and bake for 35 to 40 minutes longer. Cool. Cut into bars.

Note: For a delightful orangy flavor, add 2 teaspoons grated orange peel to filling.

Or ⅓ cup chopped and drained maraschino cherries may be added to the filling.

Stir ingredients such as coconut, grated peels, and maraschino cherries into cookie dough with a spoon; this way they will not be caught in the beaters.

Raspberry Jam Chip Bars

Makes 4½ dozen

2 cups all-purpose flour   1 egg, beaten
1 cup granulated sugar   1 cup nuts, chopped
1 teaspoon grated lemon peel   ¾ cup raspberry jam
1 cup butter, softened   ½ cup mini chocolate chips

Grease a 13 × 9 × 2-inch pan; set aside. Preheat oven to 350°F. Combine flour, sugar, and lemon peel in a bowl. Cut in butter with a pastry blender or two knives used scissor-fashion until mixture resembles coarse crumbs. Stir in beaten egg and chopped nuts, blending well. Reserve half the mixture for topping. With floured hands, press remaining mixture into the bottom of prepared pan. Spread raspberry jam over dough to within ½ inch of edges. Mix mini chocolate chips with reserved dough, and crumble over jam. Bake for 45 to 50 minutes, or until golden. Cool. Cut into bars.

Note: Raspberry Jam Chip Bars may be frozen for up to 1 month.

Pecan Pie Bars

Makes 4½ dozen

BASE

½ cup butter, softened   1 cup all-purpose flour
½ cup brown sugar, packed
  firm

FILLING

2 eggs   1 teaspoon baking powder
1 cup brown sugar, packed   1 cup pecans, chopped coarse
  firm   1 cup semisweet chocolate chips
1½ teaspoons vanilla
2 tablespoons all-purpose flour

Grease a 13 × 9 × 2-inch pan; set aside. Preheat oven to 350°F. For base, cream butter and brown sugar in a small mixing bowl on medium speed until fluffy. Lower speed, and add flour, blending well. Press dough into the bottom of prepared pan. Bake for 10 minutes. Cool for 1 hour.

Reheat oven to 350°F. For filling, beat together eggs and brown sugar in a small mixing bowl on medium speed until well blended. Add vanilla. Lower speed, and add flour and baking powder. Stir in chopped pecans with a spoon. Spread filling over cooled base; sprinkle with chocolate chips. Bake for 25 minutes, or until lightly golden. Cool. Cut into bars.

124

Sherry Walnut Treasure Bars

Makes 4 dozen

½ cup butter, softened
1 cup brown sugar, packed
  firm
1 egg
¼ cup sherry
¼ cup milk
1⅔ cups all-purpose flour,
  sifted

1 tablespoon instant coffee
½ teaspoon baking powder
½ teaspoon baking soda
¼ teaspoon cinnamon
1 cup walnuts, chopped
1 cup semisweet chocolate chips

SHERRY ICING
1 tablespoon butter, softened
2 tablespoons sherry
1 tablespoon milk

2½ cups confectioners' sugar
1 tablespoon instant coffee

TOPPING
½ cup walnuts, chopped

½ cup mini chocolate chips

    Grease a 15½ × 10½ × 1-inch jelly roll pan; set aside. Preheat oven to 375°F. Cream butter and brown sugar in a large mixing bowl on medium speed until fluffy. Beat in egg, sherry, and milk. (Batter may appear curdled, but it will smooth out when flour is added.) Lower speed and add sifted flour, instant coffee, baking powder, baking soda, and cinnamon; blend well. Stir in chopped walnuts and semisweet chocolate chips with a spoon. Spread batter in prepared pan. Bake for 20 minutes. Cool completely.

    For sherry icing, beat together butter, sherry, milk, confectioners' sugar, and instant coffee in a small mixing bowl on medium speed until smooth. Frost cooled cookies; sprinkle with chopped nuts and mini chocolate chips. Allow icing to set. Cut into bars.

Note: Do not use cooking sherry in this recipe.

Chocolate Peanut Butter Wonders

Makes 3 dozen

FILLING

1¼ *cups confectioners' sugar*
1½ *cups creamy peanut butter*
¼ *cup butter, melted*

1 *teaspoon vanilla*
¾ *cup nuts, chopped*

BASE

1½ *cups all-purpose flour*
¼ *cup unsweetened cocoa*
⅔ *cup brown sugar, packed*
    firm
½ *teaspoon baking powder*

¼ *teaspoon baking soda*
⅔ *cup butter, softened*
1 *egg, beaten*
1 *teaspoon vanilla*

TOPPING

2 *cups semisweet chocolate*
  chips

For filling, beat together confectioners' sugar, peanut butter, melted butter, and vanilla in a small mixing bowl on low speed until well blended. Stir in chopped nuts with a spoon. Set aside.

Preheat oven to 350°F. For base, stir together flour, cocoa, brown sugar, baking powder, and baking soda in a large bowl. Cut in butter with a pastry blender or two knives used scissor-fashion until mixture resembles crumbs. Stir in beaten egg and vanilla. With hands, form dough into a ball. Press dough into the bottom of an ungreased 13 × 9 × 2-inch pan. Bake for 12 to 15 minutes. Remove from oven; turn oven off. Immediately upon removing base from oven, spread with filling; sprinkle with chocolate chips. Return to warm oven for 5 minutes. Remove from oven, and spread melted chocolate chips over filling to frost. Allow chocolate to set. Cut into bars.

Chocolate Chip Toffee Bars

Makes 4½ dozen

BASE
2 cups graham cracker crumbs   ½ cup butter, melted
¼ cup granulated sugar

TOPPING
½ cup butter   1½ cups pecan halves
½ cup brown sugar, packed   ¾ cup semisweet chocolate
   firm   chips

Grease a 13 × 9 × 2-inch pan. Preheat oven to 350°F. For base, stir together graham cracker crumbs and granulated sugar in prepared pan. Pour melted butter over crumb mixture, blending well. Press mixture onto bottom of pan. Bake for 8 minutes.

Meanwhile, for topping, melt butter with brown sugar in a heavy saucepan over low heat, and bring to a boil; boil for 1 minute. Stir in pecan halves, and boil for 1 minute longer. Immediately upon removing base from oven, spread with topping. Return to oven, and bake for 15 minutes longer. Remove from oven, and sprinkle with chocolate chips; let stand for 5 minutes. Slightly swirl melted chocolate chips, leaving some chips intact. Cool. Cut into bars.

Almond Chip Cookies

Makes 5 dozen

¾ cup butter, softened   1 teaspoon baking soda
2 cups granulated sugar   ½ teaspoon cream of tartar

2 eggs
1 teaspoon almond extract
3 cups all-purpose flour, sifted

⅔ cup blanched almonds,
  chopped
⅔ cup semisweet chocolate
  chips

Grease two cookie sheets; set aside. Preheat oven to 400°F. Cream butter and sugar in a large mixing bowl on medium speed until light and fluffy. Add eggs one at a time, and almond extract. Lower speed, and add sifted flour, baking soda, and cream of tartar. Stir in chopped almonds and chocolate chips with a spoon. Drop dough by teaspoonfuls 2½ inches apart onto prepared cookie sheets. Bake for 8 to 10 minutes or until lightly golden. Cool on wire racks.

Chocolate Chip Cookies Deluxe

Makes 5 dozen

¾ cup butter, softened
¾ cup granulated sugar
½ teaspoon vanilla
1½ cups all-purpose flour

¼ cup dark rum
1½ cups ground hazelnuts
⅔ cup mini chocolate chips

Grease two cookie sheets; set aside. Preheat oven to 350°F. Cream butter and sugar in a mixing bowl on medium speed until light and fluffy. Add vanilla. Lower speed, and alternately add flour with rum, blending well. Stir in ground hazelnuts and mini chocolate chips with a spoon. Drop dough by teaspoonfuls 2 inches apart onto prepared cookie sheets. Bake for 12 to 15 minutes. Let stand on cookie sheets for 1 minute; then remove cookies to wire rack. Cool.

To assure even baking, make all the cookies in the same batch of equal size.

Chocolate Cookies

Makes 4 dozen

½ cup semisweet chocolate
 chips
1 cup butter, softened
¼ cup granulated sugar
2 eggs

1 teaspoon vanilla
2¼ cups all-purpose flour
1 teaspoon baking soda
½ cup nuts, chopped fine

Grease two cookie sheets; set aside. Preheat oven to 375°F. Melt chocolate chips in top of a double boiler over simmering water, stirring until smooth. Remove from heat. Cream butter and sugar in a large mixing bowl on medium speed until light and fluffy. Add eggs, one at a time, blending well after each addition. Blend in melted chocolate chips and vanilla. Lower speed, and add flour and baking soda. Stir in chopped nuts with a spoon. Drop dough by teaspoonfuls 2 inches apart onto prepared cookie sheets. Bake 10 to 12 minutes. Cool on wire racks.

Choco-lot Walnut Drops

Makes 4 dozen

¾ cup butter, softened
¾ cup granulated sugar
1 egg
2 tablespoons milk

1½ cups all-purpose flour,
 sifted
1 teaspoon baking powder
¾ cup walnuts, chopped

1 teaspoon vanilla
1 1-ounce square unsweetened
  chocolate, melted

½ cup semisweet chocolate
  chips
4 dozen walnut halves

Grease two cookie sheets; set aside. Preheat oven to 350°F. Cream butter and sugar in a large mixing bowl on medium speed until light and fluffy. Beat in egg, milk, vanilla, and melted unsweetened chocolate; blend well. Lower speed, and add sifted flour and baking powder. Stir in chopped walnuts and chocolate chips with a spoon. Drop dough by teaspoonfuls 2 inches apart onto prepared cookie sheets. Top each cookie with a walnut half. Bake for 15 to 18 minutes. Cool on wire rack.

Fudge Drop Cookies

Makes 5 dozen

1½ cups semisweet chocolate
  chips
2 tablespoons butter
1 15-ounce can sweetened
  condensed milk

1 teaspoon vanilla
1 cup all-purpose flour, sifted
⅔ cup nuts, chopped

Melt chocolate chips and butter with sweetened condensed milk in top of a double boiler over simmering water, stirring until smooth. Remove from heat; stir in vanilla. Beat in sifted flour, blending well. Stir in chopped nuts. Chill dough for 1 hour.

Grease two cookie sheets. Preheat oven to 325°F. Drop dough by teaspoonfuls 1½ inches apart onto prepared cookie sheets. Bake for 12 minutes. Immediately remove cookies from cookie sheets. Cool on wire racks.

Chocolate Banana Drops

Makes 6 dozen

1 cup semisweet chocolate chips
⅔ cup butter, softened
1 cup granulated sugar
2 eggs
1 teaspoon vanilla

2¼ cups all-purpose flour,
  sifted
1 cup mashed bananas
2 teaspoons baking powder
¼ teaspoon baking soda

CHOCOLATE FROSTING
⅓ cup semisweet chocolate
  chips
1 tablespoon butter
1½ cups confectioners' sugar,
  sifted

½ teaspoon vanilla
3 tablespoons milk

Preheat oven to 400°F. Melt chocolate chips in top of a double boiler over simmering water, stirring until smooth. Remove from heat. Cream butter and granulated sugar in a large mixing bowl on medium speed until light and fluffy. Beat in eggs and vanilla. Blend in melted chocolate. Lower speed, and alternately add sifted flour and mashed bananas. Add baking powder and baking soda, blending well. Drop dough by teaspoonfuls 2 inches apart onto ungreased cookie sheets. Bake for 12 to 15 minutes. Cool on wire racks.

For chocolate frosting, melt chocolate chips and butter in top of a double boiler over simmering water, stirring until smooth. Add sifted confectioners' sugar, vanilla, and milk; beat until smooth. Spread warm frosting over cooled cookies. Allow frosting to set.

Note: Chocolate Banana Drops dough will be thin.
Also, if chocolate frosting becomes too thick, add a little milk.

Remember, always preheat oven 10 to 15 minutes before baking the first batch of cookies. If the oven is not the right temperature, the cookies will spread more than they should.

Cheery Cherry Chippers

Makes 4 dozen

1 cup butter, softened
1 cup confectioners' sugar
2 teaspoons maraschino cherry juice
½ teaspoon almond extract

Few drops red food coloring
2¼ cups all-purpose flour
½ cup maraschino cherries, drained and chopped
½ cup mini chocolate chips

Preheat oven to 350°F. Beat together butter, confectioners' sugar, maraschino cherry juice, almond extract, and red food coloring in a large mixing bowl on medium speed; blend well. Lower speed, and add flour. Stir in chopped maraschino cherries and mini chocolate chips with a spoon. Drop dough by teaspoonfuls 2 inches apart onto ungreased cookie sheets. Bake for 8 to 10 minutes, or until cookies are lightly golden around the edges. Cool on wire racks.

Completely cool cookie sheets between baking batches. Cookie dough will spread if dropped on a warm cookie sheet.

Orange Walnut Chip Cookies

Makes 5½ dozen

1 cup butter, softened
½ cup granulated sugar
½ cup brown sugar, packed
    firm
1 egg
2 tablespoons orange juice

2⅓ cups all-purpose flour
½ teaspoon baking soda
2 teaspoons grated orange peel
½ cup walnuts, chopped
⅔ cup mini chocolate chips

ORANGE FROSTING

2¼ cups confectioners' sugar,
    sifted
2 tablespoons orange juice

1 tablespoon milk
1½ teaspoons grated orange
    peel

Preheat oven to 375°F. Cream butter and sugars in a large mixing bowl on medium speed until fluffy. Add egg and orange juice; blend well. Lower speed, and add flour and baking soda. Stir in orange peel, chopped walnuts, and mini chocolate chips with a spoon. Drop dough by teaspoonfuls 2 inches apart onto ungreased cookie sheets. Bake for 10 to 12 minutes. Cool on wire racks.

For orange frosting, beat sifted confectioners' sugar, orange juice, and milk in a small mixing bowl on medium speed until smooth. Stir in orange peel with a spoon. Frost cooled cookies. Allow frosting to set.

Coconut Chip Macaroons

Makes 4 dozen

3 egg whites, at room
    temperature

1 cup granulated sugar
½ teaspoon almond extract

| ¼ teaspoon salt | 2 cups flaked coconut |
| ¼ teaspoon cream of tartar | 1 cup mini chocolate chips |

Cover two cookie sheets with aluminum foil; set aside. Preheat oven to 300°F. Beat egg whites in a small mixing bowl on high speed until foamy. Add salt and cream of tartar; continue to beat until whites form soft peaks. Gradually add sugar and almond extract, beating until stiff. Gently fold in coconut and mini chocolate chips. Drop by teaspoonfuls 2 inches apart onto prepared cookie sheets. Bake for 20 minutes. Cool on cookie sheets. Carefully peel foil from macaroons.

Rum Raisin Oatmeal Chip Cookies

Makes 6 dozen

1 cup raisins	1½ teaspoons vanilla
⅓ cup dark rum	2 cups all-purpose flour
1 cup butter, softened	1 teaspoon baking soda
1 cup granulated sugar	2½ cups oatmeal
1 cup brown sugar, packed	1 cup nuts, chopped
firm	1 cup semisweet chocolate chips
2 eggs	

Soak raisins in rum in a small bowl for at least 2 hours or overnight if possible.

Grease two cookie sheets; set aside. Preheat oven to 350°F. Cream butter and sugars in a large mixing bowl on medium speed until fluffy. Beat in eggs and vanilla. Lower speed, and add flour and baking soda. Stir in oatmeal, chopped nuts, chocolate chips, and raisins—rum and all—with a spoon; blend well. Drop dough by teaspoonfuls 2 inches apart onto prepared cookie sheets. Bake for 8 to 10 minutes, or until golden. Cool on wire racks.

Note: Orange juice may be substituted for rum if preferred.

Also, toast the oatmeal for a change. Spread oatmeal on a jelly roll pan, and bake in a preheated 300°F oven for 8 to 10 minutes. Cool it before adding it to cookie dough.

Melting Lace

Makes 2 dozen

½ *cup butter*   ½ *cup brown sugar, packed*
⅓ *cup all-purpose flour*   *firm*
1 *cup quick-cooking oatmeal*   2 *tablespoons milk*

CHOCOLATE NUT FILLING
⅔ *cup semisweet chocolate*   ¼ *cup nuts, chopped fine*
   chips

Grease two cookie sheets; set aside. Preheat oven to 350°F. Melt butter in a 2-quart heavy saucepan over medium heat. Remove from heat; stir in flour, oatmeal, brown sugar, and milk, blending well. Drop batter by teaspoonfuls 2 inches apart onto prepared cookie sheets. Bake for 7 to 9 minutes, or until lightly browned. Let stand on cookie sheets for 1 minute. Then remove cookies to wire rack. Cool completely.

For chocolate nut filling, melt chocolate chips in top of a double boiler over simmering water, stirring until smooth. Add chopped nuts. Remove from heat; keep double boiler over water.

To assemble cookies, spread a layer of filling on the bottom of one cookie, and press another cookie, bottom side down, on top. Cool to set chocolate.

Chip Nut Butter Balls

Makes 4½ dozen

1 *cup butter, softened*   2 *cups ground walnuts*
⅓ *cup confectioners' sugar*   1 *cup mini chocolate chips*

2 teaspoons vanilla
2 cups all-purpose flour, sifted

1 cup confectioners' sugar,
  sifted

Cream butter and ⅓ cup confectioners' sugar in a mixing bowl on medium speed until light and fluffy. Add vanilla. Lower speed, and add sifted flour and ground walnuts. Stir in mini chocolate chips with a spoon. Chill dough for about 1 hour, or until firm.

Preheat oven to 350°F. Shape dough into 1-inch balls; place on ungreased cookie sheets. Bake for 10 to 12 minutes, or until golden. Roll cookies in 1 cup sifted confectioners' sugar while warm, then once again when they are cool.

Double Chocolate Butter Balls

Makes 4 dozen

¾ cup butter, softened
¾ cup granulated sugar
1 egg, beaten (reserve 1
  tablespoon)
1½ cups all-purpose flour,
  sifted
2 tablespoons unsweetened
  cocoa

1 teaspoon baking powder
⅔ cup mini chocolate chips
1 tablespoon water
¼ cup blanched almonds,
  chopped fine
2 tablespoons granulated sugar

Beat together butter, ¾ cup sugar, and beaten egg in a mixing bowl on medium speed until light and fluffy. Lower speed, and add sifted flour, cocoa, and baking powder. Stir in mini chocolate chips with a spoon. Chill dough for 2 hours.

Preheat oven to 375°F. Stir together reserved egg and water in a small bowl. Toss together chopped almonds and 2 tablespoons sugar in another small bowl. Shape dough into 1-inch balls; place on ungreased cookie sheets. Flatten cookies slightly with the tines of a fork that has been dipped in flour. Brush tops of cookies with egg mixture; sprinkle with almond mixture. Bake for 10 to 12 minutes. Cool on wire racks.

Mocha Bonbons

Makes 4 dozen

½ cup butter, softened   2 cups all-purpose flour, sifted
⅓ cup brown sugar, packed   ¼ cup coffee liqueur
   firm   ⅔ cup mini chocolate chips
2 egg yolks

GLAZE
1 tablespoon butter   2 tablespoons coffee liqueur
1½ cups confectioners' sugar,
   sifted

Cream butter and brown sugar in a mixing bowl on medium speed until fluffy. Add egg yolks. Lower speed, and alternately add flour with coffee liqueur, blending well. Stir in mini chocolate chips with a spoon. Chill dough for 30 minutes.

Grease two cookie sheets. Preheat oven to 350°F. Shape dough into 1-inch balls; place on prepared cookie sheets. Bake for 12 to 15 minutes. Let stand on cookie sheets for 2 minutes; then remove cookies to wire racks. Cool completely.

For glaze, melt butter in a small saucepan on low heat. Beat in sifted confectioners' sugar and coffee liqueur until smooth. Remove from heat. Quickly dip cookies into glaze; allow excess glaze to drip back into pan. (If glaze becomes too thick, return to heat and warm it, thinning with a little coffee liqueur, if necessary, until it is the desired consistency.) Allow glaze to set.

Note: Other flavored liqueurs may be substituted for coffee liqueur, if desired.

Soft cookies should be kept in a well-sealed container. A slice of apple, frequently replaced, will help keep cookies soft. Store crisp cookies in a container with a loose-fitting lid. If they soften, they can easily be recrisped by being placed in a 300°F oven for 5 minutes.

Chipperdoodles

Makes 6 dozen

1 cup butter, softened	1 teaspoon baking soda
1½ cups granulated sugar	¾ cup mini chocolate chips
2 eggs	2 tablespoons sugar
2¾ cups all-purpose flour	1 teaspoon cinnamon
2 teaspoons cream of tartar	

Preheat oven to 400°F. Cream butter and 1½ cups sugar in a large mixing bowl on medium speed until light and fluffy. Beat in eggs. Lower speed, and add flour, cream of tartar, and baking soda; blend well. Stir in mini chocolate chips with a spoon. Mix together 2 tablespoons sugar and cinnamon in a small bowl. Shape dough into 1-inch balls, and roll in sugar mixture. Place 2 inches apart on ungreased cookie sheets. Bake for 8 to 10 minutes, or until set. Immediately remove cookies from cookie sheets. Cool on wire racks.

Chocolate Oat Chews

Makes 4 dozen

⅓ cup semisweet chocolate chips	1½ teaspoons vanilla
½ cup butter, softened	¾ cup all-purpose flour, sifted
1 cup granulated sugar	1 teaspoon baking powder
1 egg	1½ cups oatmeal

Melt chocolate chips in top of a double boiler over simmering water, stirring until smooth. Remove from heat. Cream butter and sugar in a large mixing bowl on medium speed until light and fluffy. Add egg, vanilla, and melted chocolate. Lower speed, and add sifted flour and baking powder, blending well. Stir in oatmeal with a spoon. Chill dough for 30 minutes.

Grease two cookie sheets. Preheat oven to 350°F. Shape dough into ¾-inch balls. Place balls 2 inches apart on prepared cookie sheets. Bake for 10 to 12 minutes. Cool on wire racks.

Sugar Chippers

Makes 3½ dozen

⅔ cup butter, softened	1½ cups all-purpose flour
¾ cup granulated sugar	1½ teaspoons baking powder
1 egg	½ teaspoon grated lemon peel
4 teaspoons milk	½ cup mini chocolate chips
1 teaspoon vanilla	36 sugar cubes, crushed coarse

Cream butter and sugar in a mixing bowl on medium speed until light and fluffy. Beat in egg, milk, and vanilla. Lower speed, and add flour and baking powder. Stir in lemon peel and mini chocolate chips with a spoon; blend well. Chill dough for 1 hour.

Preheat oven to 375°F. Shape dough into 1-inch balls, and roll in crushed sugar cubes. Place 2 inches apart on ungreased cookie sheets. Bake for 8 to 10 minutes. Cool on wire racks.

Chocolate Wafers

Makes 5 dozen

2 cups semisweet chocolate chips	2 eggs
¾ cup butter, softened	½ teaspoon vanilla
	2½ cups all-purpose flour

1½ cups brown sugar, packed   *1 teaspoon baking soda*
   firm   *Granulated sugar*
2 tablespoons milk

Melt chocolate chips in top of a double boiler over simmering water, stirring until smooth. Remove from heat; cool for 15 minutes. Preheat oven to 350°F. Cream butter and brown sugar in a large mixing bowl on medium speed until fluffy. Beat in eggs, milk, vanilla, and melted chocolate. Lower speed, and add flour and baking soda. Cover and chill dough until easy to handle, about 1 hour. Shape dough into 1-inch balls, and roll in granulated sugar. Place 2 inches apart on ungreased cookie sheets. Slightly flatten cookies with the bottom of a glass. Bake for 9 to 12 minutes. Cool on wire racks.

Variations: These cookies are very versatile. If desired, any of the following extracts may be substituted for vanilla:

½ teaspoon almond extract   *¼ teaspoon mint extract*
1 teaspoon brandy extract   *½ teaspoon orange extract*
1 teaspoon cherry extract   *1 teaspoon rum extract*

Also, for Cream-Filled Sandwiches, try filling two Chocolate Wafers with any one of the following:

BASIC FILLING
   5 tablespoons butter, softened
   2½ cups confectioners' sugar
   2 tablespoons milk

Beat together butter, confectioners' sugar, and milk in a small mixing bowl on medium speed until smooth. Add any one of the following to achieve desired flavor.

CHERRY CREAM FILLING
   2 tablespoons maraschino cherry juice
   ½ cup confectioners' sugar (extra)

MINT CREAM FILLING
⅛ *teaspoon mint extract*
Few drops green food coloring

ORANGE CREAM FILLING
½ *teaspoon orange extract*
1 *teaspoon grated orange peel*
2 *drops yellow and 1 drop red food coloring (optional)*

VANILLA CREAM FILLING
½ *teaspoons vanilla*

Acorns

Makes 3 dozen

1 cup butter, melted
¾ cup brown sugar, packed
   firm
¾ cup pecans, chopped fine
1 teaspoon vanilla

2½ cups all-purpose flour,
   sifted
½ teaspoon baking powder
1 cup semisweet chocolate chips
¾ cup pecans, chopped fine

Preheat oven to 375°F. Beat together melted butter, brown sugar, ¾ cup chopped pecans, and vanilla in a mixing bowl on medium speed until well blended. Lower speed, and add sifted flour and baking powder; mix well. Shape dough into 1-inch balls. Slightly flatten by pressing balls onto ungreased cookie sheets; pinch tops to a point to resemble acorns. Bake for 15 minutes. Cool on wire racks.

Melt chocolate chips in top of a double boiler over simmering water, stirring until smooth. Remove from heat; keep double boiler over water. Dip large ends of cooled cookies into melted chocolate; roll in ¾ cup chopped pecans. Cool to set chocolate.

Chocolate-Covered Cherry Cookies

Makes 4 dozen

½ cup butter, softened
1 cup granulated sugar
1 egg
1½ teaspoons vanilla
1½ cups all-purpose flour

½ cup unsweetened cocoa
¼ teaspoon baking powder
¼ teaspoon baking soda
48 whole maraschino cherries,
* drained (reserve juice)*

CHOCOLATE FROSTING
1 cup semisweet chocolate chips
½ cup sweetened condensed
* milk*

4 teaspoons reserved
* maraschino cherry juice*

Preheat oven to 350°F. Cream butter and sugar in a mixing bowl on medium speed until light and fluffy. Beat in egg and vanilla. Lower speed, and add flour, cocoa, baking powder, and baking soda; blend well. Shape dough into 1-inch balls; place 2 inches apart on ungreased cookie sheets. Use thumb to make a slight indentation in center of each ball; place a maraschino cherry in each indentation. Set aside.

For chocolate frosting, melt chocolate chips with sweetened condensed milk in a small heavy saucepan over low heat stirring until smooth. Blend in maraschino cherry juice (more juice may be added, if necessary). Frost cookies, completely covering cherries. Bake for 10 minutes. Cool on wire racks.

If cookie dough is too dry, it can be moistened until it is the desired consistency by slowly adding 1 to 2 tablespoons of milk. Dough that is too soft can be stiffened by the addition of 1 to 2 tablespoons flour.

Macadamia Bites

Makes 3 dozen

½ *cup butter, softened*   1 *teaspoon vanilla*
½ *cup granulated sugar*   1½ *cups all-purpose flour*
1 *egg*   1 *5-ounce can macadamia nuts*

CHOCOLATE GLAZE
½ *cup semisweet chocolate*   2 *tablespoons butter*
   chips

Preheat oven to 350°F. Cream butter and sugar in a mixing bowl on medium speed until light and fluffy. Beat in egg and vanilla. Lower speed, and add flour (mixture will be stiff). Shape 1 teaspoonful dough around a macadamia nut, forming a ball; place 2 inches apart on ungreased cookie sheets. Bake for 10 minutes, or until lightly golden. Cool on wire racks.

For chocolate glaze, melt chocolate chips and butter in a small heavy saucepan over low heat, stirring until smooth. Spread glaze over cooled cookies. Cool to set chocolate.

Note: Hazelnuts or candied cherries may be substituted for macadamia nuts if desired.

Jelly Chip Thumbprints

Makes 3 dozen

½ *cup butter, softened*   ½ *cup mini chocolate chips*
½ *cup granulated sugar*   1 *egg white, slightly beaten*
1 *egg yolk*   ¾ *cup nuts, chopped fine*
1½ *teaspoons vanilla*   ⅓ *cup jelly*
1¼ *cups all-purpose flour,*
   sifted

Cream butter and sugar in a small mixing bowl on medium speed until light and fluffy. Beat in egg yolk and vanilla. Lower speed, and add sifted flour, blending well. Stir in mini chocolate chips with a spoon. Chill dough for 1 hour.

Preheat oven to 300°F. Shape dough into 1-inch balls; dip into beaten egg white, and roll in chopped nuts. Place 1 inch apart on ungreased cookie sheets. Gently press thumb into center of each ball; fill indentation with jelly. Bake for 20 minutes. Cool on wire racks.

Variation: For Chocolate-Filled Thumbprints, prepare cookies as directed, omitting jelly. Bake for 20 minutes; immediately upon removing cookies from oven, fill each indentation with 3 to 4 semisweet chocolate chips. Let stand for 5 minutes; then swirl melted chocolate chips to fill indentations. Allow chocolate to set.

Checkerboards

Makes 2½ dozen

⅓ cup semisweet chocolate   *1 egg*
   chips   *1 teaspoon vanilla*
⅔ cup butter, softened   *2 cups all-purpose flour*
1 cup granulated sugar   *1½ teaspoons baking powder*

Melt chocolate chips in top of a double boiler over simmering water, stirring until smooth. Remove from heat. Cream butter and sugar in a mixing bowl on medium speed until light and fluffy. Beat in egg and vanilla. Lower speed, and add flour and baking powder. Divide dough in half. Add melted chocolate chips to one-half of the dough, blending well. Roll each half of dough into two 8-inch-long logs. Place a chocolate log next to a plain log; then top with alternate logs. Press together to form a square. Wrap dough in wax paper. Freeze for 1 hour.

Preheat oven to 375°F. Using a sharp knife, cut dough into ¼-inch slices. Place slices 2 inches apart on ungreased cookie sheets. Bake for 8 to 10 minutes. Cool on wire racks.

Variations: The preceding cookie dough need not be limited to being checkerboard-shaped. Shape dough as any of the following:

CHOCOLATE-FILLED FANCIES: Roll plain dough out to a 10 × 6-inch rectangle between two sheets of wax paper. Place plain dough rectangle on a cookie sheet, and freeze for 10 minutes. Meanwhile, shape chocolate dough into a 10-inch-long log. Remove plain dough from freezer; peel off wax paper. Place chocolate log lengthwise down center of rectangle. Bring edges of plain dough up and around chocolate log; press edges of plain dough together to seal. Roll log in multicolored nonpareils. Wrap dough in wax paper. Freeze for 1 hour. Cut and bake dough as directed in preceding recipe.

HOOTY OWLS: Shape dough as directed for Chocolate-Filled Fancies; omit rolling in nonpareils. Cut dough in half crosswise. Wrap dough in wax paper. Freeze for 1 hour. Cut dough into ¼-inch slices. Place two slices, pressed together side by side, on an ungreased cookie sheet. Pinch top outsides of circles to form owl's ears. To make owl's face, place a cashew nut, curved side down, in center of cookie to represent a beak; use two semisweet chocolate chips, placed in center of chocolate circles, for eyes. Repeat procedure with remaining slices. Bake as directed in preceding recipe. Carefully remove cookies to wire racks. Cool.

CHOCOLATE ORANGE PINWHEELS: Add 1 tablespoon grated orange peel to plain dough, blending well. Roll orange dough out to a 10 × 6-inch rectangle between two sheets of wax paper. Place orange dough rectangle on a cookie sheet, and freeze for 10 minutes. Remove orange dough from freezer; peel off wax paper. Spread chocolate dough over orange dough rectangle. Starting with longer edge, roll rectangle jelly roll fashion; press edge to seal. Wrap dough in wax paper. Freeze for 1 hour. Cut and bake dough as directed in preceding recipe.

Chocolate Hazelnut Sandwiches

Makes 3 dozen

1 cup butter, softened
½ cup granulated sugar
1 cup ground hazelnuts

2 teaspoons vanilla
2 cups all-purpose flour

FILLING
1 cup semisweet chocolate chips

Cream butter and sugar in a mixing bowl on medium speed until light and fluffy. Beat in ground hazelnuts and vanilla. Lower speed, and add flour, blending well. Divide dough in half; roll into two logs 1½ inches in diameter. Wrap dough in wax paper. Chill overnight.

Grease two cookie sheets. Preheat oven to 350°F. Using a sharp knife, cut dough into ¼-inch slices. Place slices 1½ inches apart on prepared cookie sheets. Bake for 10 minutes. Cool on wire racks.

Melt chocolate chips in top of a double boiler over simmering water, stirring until smooth. Remove from heat.

To assemble cookies, spread 1 teaspoon melted chocolate onto the bottom of one cookie, and press another cookie, bottom side down, on top. Cool to set chocolate.

Peanut Butter Surprise Cookies

Makes 2½ dozen

½ cup butter, softened
½ cup creamy peanut butter
⅓ granulated sugar
⅓ cup brown sugar, packed
   firm

1½ cups all-purpose flour
½ teaspoon baking soda
3 tablespoons orange juice
⅓ cup semisweet chocolate
   chips

Beat together butter and peanut butter in a mixing bowl on medium speed. Add sugars, beating until fluffy. Lower speed, and add flour and baking soda. Blend in orange juice. Divide dough in half; roll into logs 1½ inches in diameter. Wrap dough in wax paper. Chill overnight.

Preheat oven to 350°F. Melt chocolate chips in a measuring cup in simmering water, stirring until smooth. Remove from heat. Using a sharp knife, cut dough into ¼-inch slices. Place half the slices 2 inches apart on ungreased cookie sheets. Spoon about ½ teaspoon melted chocolate onto center of each slice. Cover with remaining slices, and seal by pressing edges with the tines of a fork. Bake for 12 to 15 minutes. Let stand on cookie sheets for a few minutes; then remove cookies to wire rack. Cool.

When you make refrigerator cookies, butter is preferable to margarine because it becomes firmer than margarine when chilled, making the dough easier to slice. If refrigerator cookie dough is too soft to form, chill it for 20 minutes, then mold to desired shape. Do not despair if refrigerator cookies break while you cut them. Press them together, and they will join while baking.

Chocolate Chip
Desserts

The crowning glory of any dinner, simple to gourmet, is dessert—a chocolate dessert especially! Instead of using higher-priced chocolate in such cookery, consider the full potential of chocolate chips. They can assume many forms to grace the final course of a meal. When melted, chocolate chips can be the source of chocolate in cheesecakes, mousses, and soufflés. Left whole, they can be folded into fillings for cream puffs. Chocolate chips have found their way into recipes for pots de crème, tarts, tortes, and more, to satisfy even the nondiscerning chocolate snob. On the pages that follow you'll find a creative array of festive desserts, all using chocolate chips.

Chocolate Cheesecake

16 servings

CRUST

1¾ cups chocolate cookie crumbs	½ teaspoon nutmeg
2 tablespoons granulated sugar	⅓ cup butter, melted

CHEESE FILLING

2 cups semisweet chocolate chips	1 cup granulated sugar
3 8-ounce packages cream cheese, softened	3 eggs, at room temperature
	1½ teaspoons vanilla
	1 cup sour cream

GARNISH

1 cup whipping cream	2 tablespoons confectioners' sugar

For crust, combine chocolate cookie crumbs, granulated sugar, nutmeg, and melted butter in a 9-inch springform pan; mix until well blended. Press mixture onto the bottom and 1½ inches up sides of pan. Refrigerate until ready to use.

Preheat oven to 350°F. For cheese filling, melt chocolate chips in top of a double boiler over simmering water, stirring until smooth. Remove from heat. Beat together cream cheese and granulated sugar in a large mixing bowl on medium speed until light and fluffy. Add eggs, one at a time, blending well after each addition. Beat in melted chocolate, vanilla, and sour cream; blend until smooth. Spoon filling into crust. Bake for 1 hour, or until cheesecake is just firm when pan is gently shaken. Cool cheesecake on wire rack; do not remove metal ring from springform pan. Cover and refrigerate cheesecake overnight.

For garnish, beat whipping cream and confectioners' sugar in a chilled small bowl with chilled beaters until stiff.

To assemble dessert, remove metal ring from springform pan. Garnish cheesecake with whipped cream.

Variation: For Chocolate Almond Cheesecake, make the following changes in the preceding recipe. For crust, omit nutmeg, and instead add ¾ cup ground almonds and ½ teaspoon almond extract, increase melted butter to ½ cup; prepare crust as directed. For cheese filling, add 3 tablespoons amaretto liqueur, ½ teaspoon almond extract, and ½ cup chopped toasted almonds. Bake and cool cheesecake as directed. Garnish with sweetened whipped cream and toasted almonds.

Chocolate Chip Cheesecake

12 servings

CRUST

1½ cups graham cracker
    crumbs

6 tablespoons butter, melted

CHEESE FILLING

3 8-ounce packages cream
    cheese, softened
4 egg yolks
¾ cup granulated sugar
1 teaspoon vanilla

4 egg whites, at room
    temperature
2 teaspoons grated lemon peel
⅔ cup mini chocolate chips

TOPPING

2 cups sour cream
¼ cup granulated sugar

½ teaspoon vanilla

For crust, combine graham cracker crumbs and melted butter in a well-greased 10-inch springform pan; mix until well blended. Press mixture onto the bottom of the pan. Set aside.

Preheat oven to 350°F. For cheese filling, beat together cream cheese, egg yolks, sugar, and vanilla in a large mixing bowl on medium speed until smooth. Beat egg whites in a small mixing bowl, using clean beaters until stiff peaks form. Gently fold beaten egg whites into cheese mixture. Stir in lemon peel and mini chocolate chips. Spoon filling into crust. Bake for 40 to 50 minutes, or until slightly browned.

Meanwhile, for topping, blend together sour cream, sugar, and vanilla in a bowl. Immediately upon removing cheesecake from oven, pour topping over it, and return to oven at 475°F; bake for 5 minutes longer. Cool cheesecake on wire rack; do not remove metal ring. Refrigerate cheesecake for at least 12 hours before serving.

To serve dessert, remove metal ring from springform pan.

When a cooked cheesecake recipe calls for refrigeration, completely cool cheesecake before putting it into the refrigerator. A hot pan will break a cold glass refrigerator shelf if placed on it.

Chocolate Framboise Cheesecake

16 servings

CRUST
2½ cups chocolate cookie
   crumbs

½ cup granulated sugar
½ cup butter, melted

CHEESE FILLING
1½ cups semisweet chocolate
   chips
3 8-ounce packages cream
   cheese, softened

¾ cup granulated sugar
2 eggs, at room temperature
½ cup framboise

GARNISH
1 cup whipping cream

2 tablespoons confectioners'
   sugar

For crust, combine chocolate cookie crumbs, granulated sugar, and melted butter in a 10-inch springform pan; mix until well blended. Press mixture onto the bottom and 1 inch up the sides of the pan. Set aside.

Preheat oven to 350°F. For cheese filling, melt chocolate chips in top of a double boiler over simmering water, stirring until smooth. Remove from heat. Beat together cream cheese and granulated sugar in a large mixing bowl on medium speed until light and fluffy. Add eggs, one at a time, blending well after each addition. Add melted chocolate chips and framboise; blend well. Spoon filling into crust. Bake for 40 to 50 minutes. (Filling will be creamy in the center, but it will become firm when cool.) Turn off oven. Leave cheesecake in oven, with door ajar, for 1 hour. Remove cheesecake from oven. Cool cheesecake on wire rack; do not remove metal ring. Chill for at least 4 hours or overnight if possible.

For garnish, beat whipping cream and confectioners' sugar in a chilled small bowl with chilled beaters until stiff.

To assemble dessert, remove metal ring from springform pan. Garnish cheesecake with whipped cream rosettes.

Note: Framboise is a clear brandy distilled from raspberries. Other raspberry liqueurs may be substituted in this recipe if desired. For a variation, use another flavor of liqueur, such as almond, coffee, mint, orange, and so forth, instead of framboise.

Chocolate-Marbled Cheesecake

---

10 to 12 servings

CRUST

1¼ *cups chocolate cookie*
  crumbs
¾ *cup ground walnuts*

2 *tablespoons granulated sugar*
5 *tablespoons butter, melted*

CHEESE FILLING

½ *cup granulated sugar*
1 *envelope unflavored gelatin*
⅔ *cup milk*
2 *egg yolks, at room*
  temperature
1 *cup semisweet chocolate chips*
2 *8-ounce packages cream*
  cheese, softened

½ *cup sour cream*
1 *tablespoon grated orange peel*
2 *egg whites, at room*
  temperature
3 *tablespoons granulated sugar*

Preheat oven to 350°F. For crust, combine chocolate cookie crumbs, ground walnuts, sugar, and melted butter in an 8-inch springform pan; mix until well blended. Press mixture onto the bottom and 1 inch up the sides of the pan. Bake for 10 minutes. Cool completely; chill.

For cheese filling, combine ½ cup sugar and gelatin in a small saucepan; stir in milk until well blended. Beat in egg yolks until mixture is smooth. Let mixture stand for 3 minutes. Cook egg mixture over medium heat, stirring constantly, for about 5 minutes or until gelatin is dissolved and mixture is slightly thickened. *Do not allow to boil.* Remove from heat. Cool completely.

Melt chocolate chips in top of a double boiler over simmering water, stirring until smooth. Remove from heat; set aside. Beat cream cheese in a large mixing bowl on medium speed until smooth. Add sour cream. Lower speed, and gradually add cooled egg mixture, beating until just blended. Stir in orange peel with a spoon. Set bowl in a larger bowl filled with ice water. Chill mixture until it mounds slightly when dropped from a spoon.

Beat egg whites in a small mixing bowl on high speed until foamy. Gradually add 3 tablespoons sugar, beating until soft peaks form. Take about 2 cups of the cream cheese mixture, and blend it with the melted chocolate. Alternately spoon plain and chocolate cheese mixture into prepared crust. Swirl with a knife to marbleize. Refrigerate cheesecake for at least 4 hours or overnight if possible.

To serve cheesecake, remove metal ring from springform pan.

Pumpkin Chip Cheesecake

12 servings

CRUST

1½ cups graham cracker
  crumbs
⅓ cup ground pecans

1 teaspoon pumpkin pie spice
⅓ cup butter, melted

CHEESE FILLING

4 8-ounces packages cream
  cheese, softened
1¼ cups granulated sugar
3 tablespoons maple syrup
3 tablespoons brandy
  (optional)

1½ teaspoons pumpkin pie
  spice
4 eggs, at room temperature
1 cup canned pumpkin
¼ cup whipping cream
¾ cup mini chocolate chips

TOPPING

2 cups sour cream
¼ cup granulated sugar

1 tablespoon maple syrup
1 tablespoon brandy

GARNISH

¼ cup pecan quarters

1 tablespoon butter

Preheat oven to 425°F. For crust combine graham cracker crumbs, ground pecans, pumpkin pie spice, and melted butter in a 10-inch springform pan; mix until well blended. Press mixture onto bottom and sides of pan. Bake for 10 minutes. Remove pan from oven; reduce heat to 325°F.

For cheese filling, beat cream cheese in a large mixing bowl on medium speed until smooth. Gradually add sugar, beating until mixture is light and fluffy. Add maple syrup, brandy, and pumpkin pie spice, blending well. Add eggs, one at a time, blending well after each addition. Beat in pumpkin and whipping cream. Stir in mini chocolate chips with a spoon. Spoon filling into prepared crust. Bake for 45 minutes. (Do not open oven door during baking time.) Turn off oven; leave cheesecake, undisturbed, in oven for 1 hour. Remove cheesecake from oven.

Preheat oven to 425°F. For topping, beat together sour cream, sugar, maple syrup, and brandy in a small mixing bowl on low speed until smooth. Spread topping over cheesecake. Bake for 10 minutes. Cool cheesecake on wire rack for 1 hour. Meanwhile, for garnish, sauté pecan quarters in butter in a large heavy skillet over medium-low heat until lightly browned. Garnish cheesecake with pecans. Chill cheesecake for about 3 hours, or until firm.

To serve dessert, remove metal ring from springform pan.

Note: Pumpkin Chip Cheesecake freezes well.

To make individual cheesecakes from a standard cheesecake recipe, generously grease or line 2½-inch muffin tins, the number equaling the amount of servings in the recipe. Mix crust ingredients in a bowl until well blended. Evenly divide mixture among prepared muffin tins; firmly press onto bottoms and sides to form crusts. Set aside. Prepare cheese filling as directed, and pour into crusts. Bake for 15 to 20 minutes, or until cheesecakes are just firm when gently shaken. Cool and refrigerate cheesecakes as directed. To assemble dessert, remove cheesecakes from tins. Garnish.

Boston Cream Pie

8 servings

CUSTARD FILLING

¼ *cup granulated sugar*
2 *tablespoons cornstarch*
Dash of salt

1 *cup milk*
2 *egg yolks, beaten*
1 *teaspoon vanilla*

CAKE

1⅔ *cups all-purpose flour,*
  sifted
2 *teaspoons baking powder*
⅓ *cup butter, softened*
¾ *cup granulated sugar*

2 *egg yolks, at room*
  temperature
1½ *teaspoons vanilla*
¾ *cup milk*
2 *egg whites, at room*
  temperature

CHOCOLATE FROSTING

½ *cup semisweet chocolate*
  chips
1 *tablespoon butter*
2 *tablespoons milk*

½ *cup confectioners' sugar,*
  sifted
½ *teaspoon vanilla*

For custard filling, stir together granulated sugar, cornstarch, and salt in a heavy saucepan; gradually stir in milk. Place saucepan over medium heat, and cook, stirring constantly, until mixture comes to a boil and thickens. Slowly blend half the hot mixture into beaten egg yolks; stir egg mixture back into saucepan, blending well. Bring mixture back to a boil, and cook, stirring constantly, for 1 minute. Remove from heat. Stir in vanilla. Cover; chill.

Grease and flour two 8-inch round cake pans. Preheat oven to 350°F. For cake, stir together sifted flour and baking powder in a large bowl. Cream butter and granulated sugar in a large mixing bowl on medium speed until light and fluffy. Add egg yolks and vanilla; blend well. Lower speed, and alternately add sifted flour mixture with milk, blending until smooth. Beat egg whites in a clean bowl with clean beaters until stiff but not dry. Stir one-third of the beaten egg whites into the batter with a spoon. Gently fold in remaining whites. Pour batter into prepared pans. Bake for 30 to 35 minutes, or until cake tester inserted in center comes out clean. Cool in pans for 10 minutes; then turn cakes out onto wire racks. Cool completely.

When cakes are cool, for chocolate frosting, melt chocolate chips and butter in a heavy saucepan over low heat, stirring until smooth. Remove from heat; stir in milk. Beat in sifted confectioners' sugar and vanilla until smooth.

To assemble dessert, place one cake layer on serving plate; spread with chilled custard filling. Top with remaining layer, and pour chocolate frosting over cake, letting it drip down the sides. Refrigerate cake until ready to serve.

When adding egg yolks to a hot mixture, stir a couple of spoonfuls of the hot mixture into the yolks; blend well. Slowly stir warmed egg yolks into hot mixture. This will help prevent the yolks from cooking in lumps.

Fudge Chocolate Gateau with Chocolate Mousse Frosting

10 servings

CAKE

⅔ cup semisweet chocolate
   chips
⅓ cup butter
4 egg yolks, at room
   temperature
½ cup granulated sugar
¾ cup plus 2 tablespoons
   ground walnuts

½ cup all-purpose flour
1 teaspoon vanilla
1 tablespoon dark rum
4 egg whites, at room
   temperature
¼ cup granulated sugar

CHOCOLATE MOUSSE FROSTING

¼ cup semisweet chocolate
   chips
¾ cup whipping cream

¼ cup butter, softened
1 tablespoon dark rum

Grease a 10-inch springform pan; set aside. Preheat oven to 350°F. For cake, melt chocolate chips and butter in top of a double boiler over simmering water, stirring until smooth. Beat egg yolks and ½ cup sugar in a mixing bowl on medium speed until thick and pale. Lower speed, and add ground walnuts, flour, vanilla, rum, and melted chocolate mixture; blend well. Beat egg whites in a clean bowl with clean beaters until foamy. Gradually add ¼ cup sugar, beating until whites are stiff but not dry. Gently fold beaten egg whites into chocolate mixture. Pour batter into prepared pan. Bake for 25 to 30 minutes, or until cake tester inserted in center comes out clean. Cool cake in pan; do not remove metal ring.

For chocolate mousse frosting, place chocolate chips in a blender. Heat whipping cream in a heavy saucepan over medium-low heat, to the boiling point; pour over chocolate chips in blender. Blend for 1 minute, or until chocolate is melted. Add butter and rum; blend for 1 minute longer.

To assemble dessert, pour chocolate mousse frosting over cake, and spread evenly. Refrigerate cake until frosting is set. About 10 minutes before serving, remove cake from refrigerator; remove metal ring from springform pan.

Regal Chocolate Gateau
with Mocha Mousse Frosting

---

10 servings

CAKE

1 cup semisweet chocolate chips
½ cup butter, softened
1 cup granulated sugar
6 eggs, at room temperature

1¾ cups ground almonds
½ cup chocolate cookie crumbs
½ teaspoon baking powder
1 teaspoon vanilla

MOCHA MOUSSE FROSTING

1 cup semisweet chocolate chips
½ cup whipping cream

1 teaspoon instant coffee
1 tablespoon coffee liqueur

Grease a 10-inch springform pan; set aside. Preheat oven to 350°F. For cake, melt chocolate chips in top of a double boiler over simmering water, stirring until smooth. Remove from heat; set aside. Cream butter and sugar in a large mixing bowl on medium speed until light and fluffy. Add eggs, one at a time, blending well after each addition. Blend in melted chocolate chips. Toss together ground almonds, chocolate cookie crumbs, and baking powder; beat into chocolate mixture. Add vanilla. Pour batter into prepared pan. Bake for 45 minutes, or until cake tester inserted in center comes out clean. Cool cake in pan; do not remove metal ring.

For mocha mousse frosting, place chocolate chips in a blender. Heat whipping cream with instant coffee in a heavy saucepan over medium-low heat, bringing the mixture to the boiling point. Pour hot mixture into blender over chocolate chips. Blend for 1 minute, or until chocolate is melted. Add coffee liqueur.

To assemble dessert, remove metal ring from springform pan. Pour mocha mousse frosting over cake, carefully spreading it onto the sides. Refrigerate until frosting is set. Remove cake from refrigerator about 10 minutes before serving.

To assure that instant coffee will blend properly with the mixture it is being added to, it is important to note that instant coffee "powder" can be used in any recipe, but instant coffee "crystals" should be used only if the recipe calls for it to be dissolved in some type of liquid.

Baked Alaska

8 servings

ICE CREAM
1 pint chocolate ice cream,   1 pint vanilla ice cream,
  slightly softened   slightly softened

CAKE
1 cup all-purpose flour   1 teaspoon vanilla
¼ cup plus 2 tablespoons   1 cup mini marshmallows
  unsweetened cocoa   ½ cup nuts, chopped
½ cup butter, softened   ¾ cup semisweet chocolate
1 cup granulated sugar   chips
2 eggs, at room temperature

MERINGUE
5 egg whites, at room   Dash of cream of tartar
  temperature   ⅓ cup granulated sugar

To prepare ice cream, line four 6-ounce custard cups with plastic wrap. Spoon ½ cup softened chocolate ice cream into each cup; top chocolate ice cream with ½ cup softened vanilla ice cream; pack down ice cream with spoon. Cover and freeze until ice cream is firm.

Grease a 9-inch square pan; line bottom with wax paper. Preheat oven to 350°F.

For cake, stir together flour and cocoa in a bowl. Cream butter and sugar in a large mixing bowl on medium speed until light and fluffy. Add eggs one at a time, blending well after each addition. Add vanilla. Lower speed, and add flour mixture; blend well. Stir in marshmallows, chopped nuts, and chocolate chips with a spoon. Pour batter into prepared pan. Bake for 25 to 30 minutes, or until cake tester inserted in center comes out clean. Cool in pan for 15 minutes. Then turn cake out onto wire rack; peel off wax paper. Cool completely.

Cut cake into 4-inch squares. Remove ice cream from custard cups; peel off plastic wrap. Set one ice cream on each cake square. Freeze for about 1 hour, or until firm.

Preheat oven to 500°F. For meringue, beat egg whites and cream of tartar in a large mixing bowl on high speed until foamy. Gradually add sugar, beating until stiff peaks form. Place ice cream cakes on a cookie sheet. Evenly spread meringue over tops and sides of cakes, sealing edges to baking sheet to prevent shrinkage. Bake for 2 to 3 minutes, or until meringue is golden. Cut Baked Alaskas in half diagonally and serve immediately.

Note: Any two flavors of ice cream may be substituted.

Mint Chip Ice Cream Roll

8 to 10 servings

CAKE

2 1-ounce squares unsweetened
   chocolate
2 tablespoons butter
¾ cup all-purpose flour, sifted
½ teaspoon baking powder

¼ teaspoon salt
4 eggs, at room temperature
1 tablespoon water
1 teaspoon vanilla
1 cup granulated sugar

⅓ cup confectioners' sugar

1 quart mint chip ice cream, or any other preferred flavor,
   softened (reserve 2 tablespoons)

CHOCOLATE SAUCE

⅔ cup semisweet chocolate
   chips
1 tablespoon water

2 tablespoons butter
2 tablespoons reserved ice
   cream

Grease a 15½ × 10½ × 1-inch jelly roll pan. Line bottom of pan with wax paper; grease paper. Preheat oven to 375°F. For cake, melt unsweetened chocolate and butter in top of a double boiler over simmering water, stirring until smooth. Remove from heat; cool slightly. Stir together sifted flour, baking powder, and salt in a bowl. Beat eggs, water, and vanilla in a large mixing bowl on medium speed for about 2 minutes, or until thick and pale. Gradually add granulated sugar, 2 tablespoons at a time, beating until mixture is well blended. Fold melted chocolate into egg mixture with a spoon. Gently fold in sifted flour mixture until thoroughly blended. Evenly spread batter in prepared pan. Bake for 10 to 12 minutes, or until center of cake springs back when lightly touched.

While cake is baking, sprinkle a clean dish towel with confectioners' sugar. When cake is finished baking, turn it out onto the towel; carefully peel off wax paper. While cake is hot, roll up cake and towel together. Let stand for 1 minute; then unroll to allow steam to escape. Reroll cake and towel; cool completely.

When cake is cool, unroll it, and spread it with softened ice cream to within ½ inch of edges. Reroll cake without towel. Trim ends of roll. Wrap ice cream roll in aluminum foil. Freeze for at least 4 hours.

For chocolate sauce, melt chocolate chips with water in top of a double boiler over simmering water, stirring until smooth. Add butter and reserved ice cream; stir until well blended. (The chocolate sauce is best made 15 minutes before ice cream roll is served.)

To assemble dessert, remove foil from ice cream roll, and set on serving plate. Pour chocolate sauce over ice cream roll, and serve immediately.

Variation: For Chocolate Rum Cake Roll, fill cake with Chocolate Rum filling, page 88. Sprinkle cake roll with sifted confectioners' sugar. It is not necessary to freeze Chocolate Rum Cake Roll.

A Fool for Chips

---

6 servings

2 cups fresh raspberries,   ¼ cup water
   strawberries, or cherries   1 cup whipping cream
½ cup granulated sugar   ⅔ cup mini chocolate chips

Combine fruit, sugar, and water in a heavy saucepan over medium heat. Bring mixture to a boil; reduce heat, and simmer for 10 minutes. Remove from heat. Cool completely.

Purée cooled fruit mixture in a blender until smooth. (If using raspberries, and if desired, strain purée to remove seeds.) Taste puré for sweetness, adding sugar if necessary. Beat whipping cream in a chilled small bowl with chilled beaters, until stiff. Fold mini chocolate chips into whipped cream with a spoon. Spoon whipped cream mixture into a serving bowl. Gently fold fruit purée into whipped cream to create a marbled effect. Cover bowl, and chill for at last 2 hours.

Fresh Pears with Chocolate Sauce

---

6 servings

PEARS

Cold water	3 cups water
2 tablespoons lemon juice	1 cup granulated sugar
6 ripe pears	2 teaspoons vanilla

CHOCOLATE SAUCE

1⅓ cups semisweet chocolate chips	½ cup whipping cream
3 tablespoons hot water	1 egg white, at room temperature
1 tablespoon butter	
1 egg yolk, at room temperature	¼ cup nuts, chopped

Fill a large bowl with cold water; stir in lemon juice. Peel pears, leaving cores intact, and drop immediately into prepared water. In a 3-quart heavy saucepan over high heat, combine 3 cups water, sugar, and vanilla; bring to a boil. When sugar is dissolved, add pears. Reduce heat to medium, and poach pears for about 25 minutes, or until tender. Remove from heat; cool pears in poaching liquid. (Pears may be poached several hours or a day before being served.)

For chocolate sauce, melt chocolate chips with hot water in top of a double boiler over simmering water, stirring until smooth. Remove from heat; stir in butter, blending until melted. Beat in egg yolk and whipping cream; set aside. Beat egg white in a small mixing bowl on high speed until stiff peaks form. Gently fold warm chocolate mixture into beaten egg white.

To assemble dessert, place poached pears on individual serving dishes. Spoon warm chocolate sauce over pears; sprinkle with chopped nuts.

Chocolate Fondue

---

6 to 8 servings

2 cups semisweet chocolate chips

¾ cup whipping cream

Melt chocolate chips with whipping cream in top of a double boiler over simmering water, stirring until smooth. Pour mixture into a fondue pot, and keep warm over a low flame.

Variation: Any one of the following may be added to Chocolate Fondue:

½ cup ground nuts
1 tablespoon instant coffee
2 tablespoons kirsch, or other preferred liqueur

½ teaspoon cinnamon, or other preferred spice
¼ teaspoon mint extract, or other preferred extract

Dipping Suggestions: Fruits such as apples, bananas, maraschino cherries, pineapple chunks, and strawberries may be used. Cakes such as pound cake, angel cake, or sponge cake cut into bite-size pieces are also good. Marshmallows are great, too.

Note: Toss apple and banana slices in lemon juice to prevent browning. To keep Chocolate Fondue from burning, use a candle flame. Do *not* use Sterno, butane, or alcohol burners.

Chocolate Chip-Filled Cream Puffs

---

1 dozen

CREAM PUFF PASTRY

1 cup hot water
½ cup butter
1 tablespoon granulated sugar

¼ teaspoon salt
1 cup all-purpose flour, sifted
4 eggs, at room temperature

CHOCOLATE CHIP FILLING

½ cup confectioners' sugar,
sifted
¼ cup plus 1 tablespoon
unsweetened cocoa

2 cups whipping cream
2 teaspoons vanilla
1 cup mini chocolate chips

CHOCOLATE GLAZE

½ cup semisweet chocolate
chips
3 tablespoons butter

1½ cups confectioners' sugar,
sifted
3 tablespoons boiling water

Lightly grease a cookie sheet; set aside. Preheat oven to 450°F. For cream puff pastry, bring hot water, butter, granulated sugar, and salt in a saucepan over medium heat to a rolling boil. Add sifted flour all at once. Using a wooden spoon, vigorously beat mixture until it leaves the sides of the saucepan and forms a smooth ball. Remove from heat. Quickly add eggs, one at a time, beating until smooth after each addition. Continue to beat mixture until it is well blended. Drop dough by tablespoonfuls 2 inches apart onto prepared cookie sheet. Bake for 15 minutes. Reduce heat to 350°F; bake for 15 to 20 minutes longer, or until golden. Remove pastry to wire rack. Cool completely.

For chocolate chip filling, stir together sifted confectioners' sugar and cocoa in a bowl. Beat whipping cream, confectioners' sugar mixture, and vanilla in a chilled small bowl with chilled beaters until stiff. Fold in mini chocolate chips with a spoon. Chill until ready to use.

For chocolate glaze, melt semisweet chocolate chips and butter in top of a double boiler over simmering water, stirring until smooth. Remove from heat; beat in sifted confectioners' sugar and boiling water, blending until smooth.

To assemble dessert, cut off the tops of the cream puffs, and scoop out dough in center; discard dough. Fill shells with chocolate chip filling. Replace tops, and frost with chocolate glaze. Refrigerate until ready to serve.

Note: Instead of chocolate chip filling, the cream puffs may be filled with Chocolate Rum Filling, page 88.

Chocolate Mousse

---

8 servings

1⅓ cups semisweet chocolate chips	1 tablespoon dark rum
	½ teaspoon vanilla
2 tablespoons water	6 egg whites, at room
¼ cup confectioners' sugar	temperature
½ cup butter, cut into pieces	2 tablespoons granulated sugar
6 egg yolks, beaten	

GARNISH

1 cup whipping cream	¼ teaspoon rum extract
2 tablespoons confectioners' sugar	(optional)

Melt chocolate chips with water in top of a double boiler over simmering water, stirring until smooth. Add confectioners' sugar. Stir in butter, one piece at a time, blending until melted. Slowly blend half the chocolate mixture into beaten egg yolks; stir egg mixture back into chocolate mixture in double boiler, blending well. Remove from heat; stir in rum and vanilla. Beat egg whites in a large mixing bowl on high speed until foamy. Gradually add granulated sugar, beating until stiff peaks form. Gently fold chocolate mixture into beaten egg whites. Pour mousse into individual serving dishes. Refrigerate for at least 4 hours.

For garnish, beat whipping cream, confectioners' sugar, and rum extract in a chilled small bowl with chilled beaters until stiff.

To serve dessert, garnish each mousse with whipped cream.

To delight guests, serve mousse in edible chocolate cups. To make chocolate cups, line muffin tins with foil liners. Melt ¼ cup semi-sweet chocolate chips per chocolate cup desired in top of a double boiler over simmering water, stirring until smooth. Remove from heat; keep double boiler over water. Using a small pastry brush or teaspoon, coat bottoms and sides of prepared tins with melted chocolate chips to about ¼ inch thick. Refrigerate chocolate cups until firm. Before filling chocolate cups with mousse, carefully peel off foil liners.

Chocolate Cherry Mousse

4 servings

1⅓ cups semisweet chocolate chips	*¾ cup confectioners' sugar*
2 tablespoons hot water	*3 tablespoons kirsch*
1 cup whipping cream	*½ cup sour cream*
	4 whole maraschino cherries

Melt chocolate chips with hot water in top of a double boiler over simmering water, stirring until smooth. Remove from heat. Beat whipping cream and confectioners' sugar in a chilled small bowl with chilled beaters until stiff. Fold melted chocolate mixture and kirsch into whipped cream, blending until smooth. Gently fold in sour cream. Spoon mousse into individual dessert dishes; garnish each with a maraschino cherry. Refrigerate until ready to serve.

Note: Other liqueurs may be substituted for kirsch if desired.

Easy Chocolate Pots de Crème

6 servings

1¼ cups light cream
1 cup semisweet chocolate chips

2 egg yolks, at room
   temperature
3 tablespoons brandy

    Scald light cream in a small heavy saucepan over medium-low heat. Meanwhile, combine chocolate chips, egg yolks, and brandy in a blender. Pour scalded cream into blender, and blend until chocolate is melted and smooth. Pour mixture into crème pots or demitasse cups. Cover and chill for at least 3 hours.

Note: Dark rum or liqueurs may be substituted for brandy if desired.

Chocolate Soufflé

12 to 14 servings

2 envelopes unflavored gelatin
½ cup water
⅔ cups crème de cacao liqueur
½ cup granulated sugar
2 cups semisweet chocolate
   chips
8 egg yolks, at room
   temperature

8 egg whites, at room
   temperature
Dash of salt
¾ cup granulated sugar
2 cups whipping cream
½ cup pistachio nuts or
   almonds, chopped

    To make a collar for a 2-quart soufflè dish, first tear a piece of aluminum foil 4 to 6 inches longer than the dish's circumference. Fold foil in half lengthwise. Fit foil around the outside of the soufflè dish, extending 3 inches above the top, and secure with a string tied 2 to 3 inches above the base of the dish. Set aside.

Sprinkle gelatin over water and crème de cacao in a 2-quart heavy saucepan; let stand for 5 minutes. Add ½ cup sugar to gelatin mixture, and place over low heat. Cook, stirring constantly, until gelatin and sugar dissolve. Add chocolate chips, and stir until melted. Remove from heat. Beat in egg yolks, one at a time, until well blended. Cool completely.

Beat egg whites and salt in a large mixing bowl on high speed, until foamy. Gradually add ¾ cup sugar, beating until stiff peaks form. Gently fold one-third of the beaten egg whites into cooled chocolate mixture; then fold in remaining whites. Beat whipping cream in a chilled small bowl with clean, chilled beaters until stiff. Fold whipped cream into chocolate mixture. Spoon mixture into prepared soufflé dish. Chill for several hours or overnight if possible.

To serve dessert, carefully remove foil collar from dish and garnish soufflé with chopped nuts.

Note: Amaretto, coffee, or other liqueurs may be substituted for crème de cacao if desired.

To blend beaten egg whites evenly into another mixture (such as chocolate in soufflé), add them one-third at a time, gently folding until no white streaks remain.

Chocolate Coconut Soufflé

6 servings

4 ounces cream cheese, softened
½ cup milk
⅔ cup semisweet chocolate chips
4 egg yolks, beaten
½ cup flaked coconut

1 teaspoon vanilla
4 egg whites, at room temperature
¼ cup confectioners' sugar, sifted

Beat cream cheese and milk in a small mixing bowl on medium speed until smooth. Melt chocolate chips with beaten cream cheese mixture in a heavy saucepan over low heat, stirring until smooth. Slowly blend a spoonful of the chocolate mixture into beaten egg yolks; stir egg mixture back into saucepan, blending well. Continue cooking, stirring constantly, until mixture thickens. Stir in coconut and vanilla. Remove from heat; cool completely.

Preheat oven to 325°F. Beat egg whites in a large mixing bowl on high speed until soft peaks form. Gradually add sifted confectioners' sugar, beating until stiff peaks form. Gently fold cooled chocolate mixture into beaten egg whites. Pour mixture into an ungreased 1-quart soufflé dish or casserole; set in a pan of hot water. Bake for 1 hour, or until a sharp knife inserted into soufflé comes out clean. Serve immediately.

Note: A baked soufflé that falls can easily be saved by being served in individual dessert dishes and being called mousse.

Frozen Orange Chip Soufflé

10 servings

2 envelopes unflavored gelatin
2 cups fresh orange juice
3 tablespoons grated orange
   peel
1 teaspoon grated lemon peel
2 drops red food coloring
6 drops yellow food coloring

4 egg yolks, at room
   temperature
½ cup granulated sugar
4 egg whites, at room
   temperature
½ cup granulated sugar
2 cups whipping cream
1 cup mini chocolate chips

Make a collar for a 1-quart soufflé dish (see instructions on page 168). Set aside.

Sprinkle gelatin over orange juice in top of a double boiler; let stand for 5 minutes. Stir in orange peel, lemon peel, and red and yellow food colorings, blending well. Beat egg yolks with a wire whisk for about 3 minutes, or until thick and pale. Gradually beat in ½ cup sugar. Stir beaten egg yolks into gelatin mixture in double boiler; blend well. Place double boiler over simmering water, and cook, stirring constantly, for about 15 minutes, or until gelatin dissolves and mixture thickens. Remove from heat, and pour mixture into a bowl set inside a larger bowl filled with ice water. Cool gelatin mixture, stirring occasionally, for 15 minutes; then stir constantly until mixture thickens and mounds when dropped from a spoon. Beat egg whites in a large mixing bowl on high speed until foamy. Gradually add ½ cup sugar, beating until stiff peaks form. Gently fold gelatin mixture into beaten egg whites. Beat whipping cream in a chilled small bowl with clean, chilled beaters until stiff. Fold whipped cream into gelatin mixture. Fold in mini chocolate chips. Spoon mixture into prepared soufflé dish. Freeze soufflé for about 4 hours, or until firm.

To serve dessert, remove soufflé from freezer 15 minutes before serving. Carefully remove foil collar from dish.

Note: Frozen Orange Chip Soufflé may be prepared 1 day in advance and frozen overnight if desired.

Chocolate Almond Tart
with Chocolate Mousse Filling

---

10 servings

CHOCOLATE ALMOND TART

½ cup butter, softened
¼ cup granulated sugar
1 egg, at room temperature
¼ teaspoon almond extract

1 cup all-purpose flour
½ cup almonds, chopped
¼ cup semisweet chocolate
  chips, chopped

CHOCOLATE MOUSSE FILLING

1⅓ cups semisweet chocolate
  chips
1 cup whipping cream

4 egg yolks, at room
  temperature
2 tablespoons crème de cacao
  liqueur
1 teaspoon vanilla

GARNISH

1 cup whipping cream
1 tablespoon confectioners'
  sugar

1 tablespoon crème de cacao
  liqueur

Grease a 10-inch springform pan; set aside. Preheat oven to 350°F. For chocolate almond tart, cream butter and granulated sugar in a large mixing bowl on medium speed until light and fluffy. Beat in egg and almond extract. Lower speed, and add flour, blending well. Stir in chopped almonds and chocolate chips with a spoon. Pat dough onto bottom of prepared pan; if dough becomes too sticky, flour fingertips. Bake for about 25 minutes, or until top is slightly browned. Cool completely.

For chocolate mousse filling, place chocolate chips in a blender. Heat whipping cream in a heavy saucepan over medium-low heat to the boiling point. Pour hot cream into blender, and blend for 1 minute, or until chocolate is melted and smooth. Add egg yolks, crème de cacao, and vanilla; blend for 1 minute longer. Pour filling onto prepared crust. Refrigerate until firm.

For garnish, beat whipping cream, confectioners' sugar, and crème de cacao in a chilled small bowl with chilled beaters until stiff.

To assemble dessert, remove metal ring from springform pan. Garnish tart with whipped cream rosettes.

Chocolate Brownie Tart

8 to 10 servings

CRUST

1 cup all-purpose flour
¼ cup brown sugar, packed firm
1 1-ounce square unsweetened chocolate, grated

½ cup butter, softened
2 tablespoons milk
1 teaspoon vanilla

BROWNIE FILLING

3 1-ounce squares unsweetened chocolate
½ cup semisweet chocolate chips
½ cup butter, cut into pieces

1½ cups granulated sugar
3 eggs, at room temperature
2 teaspoons vanilla
¾ cup all-purpose flour
½ cup nuts, chopped

CHOCOLATE ICING
²/₃ cup semisweet chocolate   ¼ cup butter
   chips   2 teaspoons oil

For crust, combine flour, brown sugar, and grated unsweetened chocolate in a large bowl. Cut in butter with a pastry blender or two knives used scissor-fashion until mixture resembles coarse crumbs. Using a fork, mix in milk and vanilla, stirring until just blended. Pat dough onto the bottom and sides of an ungreased 11-inch tart pan with a removable bottom; if dough becomes too sticky, flour fingertips. Set aside.

Preheat oven to 350°F. For brownie filling, melt chocolates in top of a double boiler over simmering water, stirring until smooth. Remove from heat. Stir in butter, one piece at a time, blending until melted. Transfer chocolate mixture to a large mixing bowl. Beat in granulated sugar on medium speed; blend well (mixture will be granular). Add eggs, one at a time, blending well after each addition. Add vanilla. Lower speed, and add flour, ¼ cup at a time, blending well after each addition. Stir in chopped nuts with a spoon. Pour filling into crust. Bake for 20 to 25 minutes, or until cake tester inserted in center comes out clean. Cool completely.

For chocolate icing, combine chocolate chips, butter, and oil in top of a double boiler over simmering water. Beat mixture with a wire whisk until melted and smooth. Cool icing, whisking occasionally, until it is a spreadable consistency.

To assemble dessert, spread icing over tart; let stand until icing is set. Remove tart from pan and serve.

Jonathan's Nut and Chip Tart

---

10 servings

CRUST
⅓ cup butter, softened
¼ cup granulated sugar

1 egg yolk, at room
   temperature
1 cup all-purpose flour

FILLING
⅔ cup brown sugar, packed
   firm
¼ cup butter
¼ cup light corn syrup
2 tablespoons whipping cream

2 cups walnuts, chopped coarse
½ teaspoon rum extract
½ cup semisweet chocolate
   chips

GARNISH
1 cup whipping cream
2 tablespoons confectioners'
   sugar

¼ teaspoon rum extract

Preheat oven to 375°F. For crust, cream softened butter and granulated sugar in a small mixing bowl on medium speed until light and fluffy. Add egg yolk, blending well. Lower speed, and add flour (mixture will be crumbly). With hands, form dough into a ball. Press dough onto the bottom and sides of an ungreased 9-inch tart pan with a removable bottom. Bake for 12 minutes, or until light golden. Cool completely.

Preheat oven to 375°F. For filling, combine brown sugar, butter, corn syrup, and whipping cream in a 2-quart heavy saucepan on medium-low heat. Cook, stirring constantly, until mixture comes to a full boil; boil for 1 minute. Add chopped walnuts, stirring until well blended. Remove from heat; stir in rum extract. Pour filling into prepared crust, spreading evenly. Sprinkle chocolate chips over filling. Bake for 10 minutes. Cool.

For garnish, beat whipping cream, confectioners' sugar, and rum extract in a chilled small mixing bowl with chilled beaters until stiff. Chill until ready to use.

To assemble dessert, remove tart from pan. Garnish tart with whipped cream.

French Chocolate Torte

---

12 servings

CAKE

1 cup semisweet chocolate chips	¾ cup butter, softened
1½ cups ground pecans	¾ cup granulated sugar
2 tablespoons all-purpose flour	6 egg yolks, at room temperature
	6 egg whites, at room temperature

FROSTING

⅔ cup semisweet chocolate chips	2 teaspoons instant coffee
¼ cup hot water	2 egg yolks, at room temperature
¼ cup granulated sugar	1 cup whipping cream

Cover bottom of a 10-inch springform pan with wax paper; grease and flour paper. Preheat oven to 350°F. For cake, melt chocolate chips in top of a double boiler over simmering water, stirring until smooth. Remove from heat; cool to room temperature. Toss together ground pecans and flour in a bowl. Cream butter and sugar in a large mixing bowl on medium speed until light and fluffy. Add egg yolks, one at a time, blending well after each addition. Lower speed, and add melted chocolate chips and ground pecan mixture. Beat egg whites in a large mixing bowl, using clean beaters until stiff peaks form. Gently fold beaten egg whites into chocolate mixture, blending thoroughly. Pour batter into prepared pan. Bake for 30 minutes, or until cake tester inserted in center comes out clean. Cool completely.

For frosting, melt chocolate chips with hot water, sugar, and instant coffee in a heavy saucepan over low heat, stirring until smooth. Remove from heat; cool mixture, stirring occasionally, for 5 minutes. Beat in egg yolks, one at a time, with a wire whisk, blending well after each addition. Let mixture cool to room temperature. Beat whipping cream in a chilled small bowl with chilled beaters until stiff. Fold whipped cream into chocolate mixture. Chill frosting for about 20 minutes, or until it is a spreadable consistency.

To assemble dessert, remove metal ring from springform pan; remove bottom of pan from cake; peel away wax paper. Set cake on a serving plate, and frost. Chill torte for at least 2 hours before serving.

Ladyfinger Torte

6 to 8 servings

TORTE

2 cups milk

3 tablespoons dark rum

4 packages ladyfingers, split
  lengthwise

1⅓ cups semisweet chocolate
  chips

1 cup butter, softened

2 cups confectioners' sugar

2 eggs, at room temperature

1 tablespoon instant coffee

⅔ cup toasted almonds,
  chopped

GARNISH

1 cup whipping cream

¼ cup confectioners' sugar

1 tablespoon dark rum

⅓ cup mini chocolate chips

For torte, stir together milk and rum in a bowl. Dip in milk mixture the amount of split ladyfingers needed to line the bottom and sides of a 9-inch springform pan. Set aside. Melt chocolate chips in top of a double boiler over simmering water, stirring until smooth. Remove from heat; cool slightly. Cream butter and confectioners' sugar in a large mixing bowl on medium speed until light and fluffy. Add eggs, one at a time, blending well after each addition. Beat in melted chocolate chips and instant coffee. Stir in chopped almonds with a spoon. Fill prepared pan with alternate layers of chocolate mixture and remaining ladyfingers. Chill torte for at least 4 hours.

For garnish, beat whipping cream, confectioners' sugar, and rum in a chilled small bowl with chilled beaters, until stiff.

To assemble dessert, remove metal ring from springform pan.

Garnish torte with whipped cream; decorate with mini chocolate chips.

Sacher Torte

16 servings

CAKE

1½ cups semisweet chocolate   ¾ cup sugar
   chips   ¾ cup all-purpose flour, sifted
½ cup butter, cut into pieces   6 egg whites, at room
1½ teaspoons vanilla   temperature
6 egg yolks, at room   Dash of salt
   temperature

APRICOT GLAZE

1 cup apricot preserves

CHOCOLATE GLAZE

1 cup semisweet chocolate chips   5 tablespoons butter

    Grease and flour a 9-inch springform pan; set aside. Preheat oven to 350°F. For cake, melt chocolate chips in top of a double boiler over simmering water, stirring until smooth. Remove from heat. Stir in butter, one piece at a time, blending until smooth. Add vanilla. Cool completely.

    Beat egg yolks with ¼ cup sugar in a large mixing bowl on medium speed until thick and pale. Add remaining sugar, ¼ cup at a time, and continue to beat until mixture is light and fluffy. Lower speed, and beat in cooled chocolate mixture. Fold in sifted flour. Beat egg whites and salt in a clean large bowl with clean beaters until soft peaks form. Stir about one-quarter of the beaten egg whites into the chocolate mixture; blend well. Gently fold in remaining whites, blending until no white streaks remain. Pour batter into prepared pan. Bake for 45 to 50 minutes, or until cake tester inserted in center comes out clean. Cool cake in pan for 15 minutes; then remove metal ring. Cool completely.

    When cake is cool, use a serrated knife to cut a very thin slice from top of the cake, removing crust. Slice cake into thirds horizontally; set aside.

    For apricot glaze, melt apricot preserves in a small heavy sauce-

pan over medium-low heat, stirring occasionally. Pour melted preserves into a strainer, and push through with a spoon. Keep apricot
glaze warm.

For chocolate glaze, melt chocolate chips and butter in top of a
double boiler over simmering water, stirring until smooth. Keep
chocolate glaze warm.

To assemble dessert, place a layer of cake on a serving plate, and
spread with ¼ cup warm apricot glaze. Top with second layer;
spread with ¼ cup apricot glaze. Place remaining cake layer on
top, and spread top and sides of cake with remaining apricot glaze.
Pour chocolate glaze over cake, evenly spreading over top and
sides. Allow chocolate to set.

Note: Traditionally, Sacher Tortes are decorated by writing the
word *Sacher* in chocolate on the top of them. See directions for
Chocolate Writing, page 32.

Strawberry Meringue Cream Torte

---

8 to 10 servings

MERINGUE LAYERS

4 egg whites, at room   Dash of salt
   temperature   1 cup granulated sugar
¼ teaspoon cream of tartar

FILLING

1 cup semisweet chocolate chips   ¼ cup confectioners' sugar
3 tablespoons butter   2 cups fresh strawberries
2 cups whipping cream

GARNISH

1 cup reserved whipped cream   ½ cup fresh strawberries

Draw three 8-inch circles on wax paper; place on cookie sheets.
Preheat oven to 250°F. For meringue layers, beat egg whites, cream
of tartar, and salt in a small mixing bowl on high speed until
foamy. Gradually add granulated sugar, beating until stiff peaks
form. Divide meringue into thirds, and evenly spread onto wax paper circles. Bake for 45 minutes, or until meringue is dry and lightly
colored. Cool.

For filling, melt chocolate chips and butter in top of a double boiler over simmering water, stirring until smooth. Remove from heat; cool. Beat whipping cream and confectioners' sugar in a chilled small bowl with chilled beaters until stiff; reserve 1 cup whipped cream for garnish. Wash and slice 2 cups strawberries.

To assemble dessert, carefully peel wax paper from meringue layers. Place one meringue layer on a serving plate, and spread it with half the melted chocolate. Spread chocolate with half the whipped cream, and arrange 1 cup sliced strawberries on top. Place second meringue layer on top of the filling, and repeat procedure. Top with third meringue layer. Garnish torte with reserved whipped cream and ½ cup whole strawberries. Refrigerate torte for at least 4 hours, but no more than 8 hours.

Note: Fresh raspberries may be substituted for strawberries if desired. They may be left whole when used in filling.

Viennese Torte

12 to 14 servings

CAKE

½ cup granulated sugar
6 egg yolks, at room
  temperature
¼ teaspoon salt
1 teaspoon vanilla

1 cup all-purpose flour, sifted
1 cup pecans, chopped fine
6 egg whites, at room
  temperature
¼ cup granulated sugar

CREAM FILLING

1 cup semisweet chocolate chips
¾ cup butter, softened
1¼ cups confectioners' sugar,
  sifted

Dash of salt
1 egg, at room temperature
3 tablespoons dark rum

FROSTING

½ cup granulated sugar
2 tablespoons cornstarch
Dash of salt
½ cup boiling water

1 1-ounce square unsweetened
  chocolate
1½ tablespoons butter
½ cup pecans, chopped fine

Grease three 8-inch round pans; line bottoms with wax paper. Preheat oven to 350°F. For cake, beat together ½ cup granulated sugar, egg yolks, salt, and vanilla in a large mixing bowl on medium speed for about 5 minutes, or until light and fluffy. Lower speed and add sifted flour and chopped pecans, blending well. Beat egg whites in a clean large bowl with clean beaters, until foamy. Gradually add ¼ cup granulated sugar, beating until stiff peaks form. Gently fold beaten egg whites into egg yolk mixture. Divide batter among prepared pans. Bake for 20 to 25 minutes, or until cake tester inserted in center comes out clean. Cool in pans for 10 minutes; then turn cakes out onto wire racks. Cool completely.

For cream filling, melt chocolate chips in top of a double boiler over simmering water, stirring until smooth. Remove from heat; cool, stirring occasionally. Beat butter in a mixing bowl on medium speed until fluffy. Lower speed, and add sifted confectioners' sugar and salt. Increase speed to medium-high, and beat mixture for about 6 minutes, or until very light and fluffy. Add egg, and continue to beat until smooth. Quickly fold melted chocolate and rum into mixture. Chill filling until slightly stiffened.

For frosting, combine granulated sugar, cornstarch, and salt in a heavy saucepan; slowly stir in boiling water, blending well. Place saucepan over medium-low heat, and cook, stirring constantly, until mixture is smooth and thickened. Add unsweetened chocolate and butter; continue cooking until melted and smooth. Set top of double boiler in a bowl filled with ice water, and chill frosting until it is a spreadable consistency.

To assemble dessert, place first cake layer on a serving plate, and spread one-third of the cream filling on top. Place second layer on top of filling, and repeat procedure. Place third cake layer on top, and spread with remaining cream filling; sprinkle top with chopped pecans. Chill cake until filling is firm. Before frosting cake, scrape excess filling from sides. Frost only the sides of the cake. Refrigerate torte for several hours before serving.

Pies Made with Chocolate Chips

Imagine Jack Horner's elation if he had pulled out a chocolate chip from his pie! Now anyone can experience this joy. All the pies in this chapter use chocolate chips in one form or another. There are a number of sumptuous cream, custard, and nut pies with whole or melted chips blended throughout; in other recipes chocolate chips are nestled in crumb crusts or suspended in light and luscious chiffon fillings. Recipes for cool and creamy frozen pies, tailor-made for warm summer evenings, also can be found. Choose a recipe, and experience the tantalizing results of pie enhanced by chocolate chips—used in novel ways.

PIECRUST TABLE AND RECIPES

The following piecrust tables and recipes will be referred to throughout this chapter. Also included are some tips on making crumb crusts and pastry shells. The tastes of individual cooks vary, so feel free to experiment with piecrust and filling combinations. (However, do not substitute crumb crusts for partially baked or unbaked pastry shells in recipes calling for the latter two.)

• For homemade chocolate cookie crumbs, see Chocolate Cookies, page 128. Prepare dough as directed. Spread dough in a greased 13 × 9 × 2-inch pan. Bake for 20 minutes. Crumble while warm. Chocolate cookie crumbs freeze well.

• An easy way to crumble cookies or graham crackers is to put a few at a time into a plastic bag and crush them with a rolling pin.

• To remove pieces of crumb crust pie from a pie plate easily, rub the outside of the plate with a warm, damp towel before serving. This will soften the butter in the crust, making it less likely to stick to the plate.

• For light and flaky pastry shells, handle dough as little as possible.

• Avoid stretching dough when fitting it into the pie plate. If the dough is stretched, the pastry shell will shrink during baking.

• Besides pricking the pastry shell with a fork, weighing it down during baking also helps prevent shrinking and puffing. To do so, gently cover prepared unbaked shell with aluminum foil; fill it with dried beans or pie weights. Bake pastry shell for 5 minutes. Carefully remove foil and beans or weights, and continue to bake as directed. (The beans can be reused.)

Chocolate Cookie Crumb Crust

Size of Crust	Cups of Crumbs	Tablespoons of Sugar	Cups of Melted Butter
8-inch	1¼	0 to 2	¼
9-inch	1½	0 to 4	⅓

Toss together chocolate cookie crumbs and sugar in desired size pie plate. Pour melted butter over crumbs; mix until well blended. Press mixture onto the bottom and sides of pie plate. Chill until ready to fill.

Note: For Baked Chocolate Cookie Crumb Crust, bake in preheated 350°F oven for 5 to 8 minutes. Cool before filling.

Variations: Any of the following may be added to the Chocolate Cookie Crumb Crust.

CHOCOLATE CINNAMON CRUMB CRUST
¼ to ½ teaspoon cinnamon

CHOCOLATE MINT CRUMB CRUST
¼ teaspoon mint extract

CHOCOLATE NUT CRUMB CRUST
Reduce chocolate cookie crumbs by ¼ cup,
add ¼ cup fine chopped nuts or ½ cup ground nuts

CHOCOLATE ORANGE CRUMB CRUST
1 tablespoon grated orange peel

MOCHA CRUMB CRUST
1 to 2 teaspoons instant coffee powder

Graham Cracker Crumb Crust

Size of Crust	Cups of Crumbs	Tablespoons of Sugar	Cups of Melted Butter
8-inch	1¼	2	¼
9-inch	1½	4	⅓

Toss together graham cracker crumbs and sugar in desired size pie plate. Pour melted butter over crumb mixture; mix until well blended. Press mixture onto the bottom and sides of pie plate. Chill until ready to fill.

Note: For Baked Graham Cracker Crumb Crust, bake in preheated 375°F oven for 5 to 8 minutes. Cool before filling.

Variations: Any of the following may be added to the Graham Cracker Crumb Crust.

GRAHAM COCOA CRUMB CRUST
1 to 2 tablespoons unsweetened cocoa

GRAHAM SPICE CRUMB CRUST
¼ to ½ teaspoon desired spice

GRAHAM ORANGE CRUMB CRUST
2 to 3 teaspoons grated orange peel

Ground Nut Crust

Makes 8- or 9-inch crust

1½ cups ground nuts   *2 tablespoons granulated sugar*

Preheat oven to 400°F. Toss together ground nuts and sugar in desired size pie plate. Firmly press mixture with a spoon onto the bottom and sides of pie plate. Bake for 8 minutes. Cool completely before filling.

Chocolate Coconut Crust

Makes 9-inch crust

2 cups flaked coconut   *2 tablespoons butter*
1 cup semisweet chocolate chips   *1 tablespoon light corn syrup*

Grease a 9-inch pie plate. Preheat oven to 150°F. Place coconut in prepared pie plate, and warm in oven while preparing other ingredients. Melt chocolate chips and butter with corn syrup in top of a double boiler over simmering water, stirring until smooth. Remove coconut from oven. Pour melted chocolate mixture over warmed coconut, and mix with a fork until thoroughly blended. Firmly press chocolate and coconut mixture with a spoon onto bottom and sides of pie plate. Chill until ready to fill.

Chocolate Crunch Crust

Makes 9-inch crust

½ cup semisweet chocolate   *2 tablespoons butter*
   chips   *1¾ cups crispy rice cereal*

Grease a 9-inch pie plate; set aside. Melt chocolate chips and butter in top of a double boiler over simmering water, stirring until smooth. Remove from heat. Stir in rice cereal, blending well. Press mixture with a spoon onto bottom and sides of prepared pie plate. Chill until ready to fill.

Pastry Shell

Makes 8- or 9-inch shell

1¼ cups all-purpose flour   *⅓ cup lard or shortening*
Dash of salt   *3 to 4 tablespoons ice water*

Toss together flour and salt in a bowl. Cut in lard with a pastry blender or two knives used scissor-fashion until mixture resembles coarse crumbs. Sprinkle 1 tablespoon of ice water over mixture; gently toss with a fork. Repeat procedure, blending until mixture is just moistened. With hands, form dough into a ball. Slightly flatten ball with hands on a lightly floured surface. Using a well-floured rolling pin, evenly roll dough from center to edges into a circle approximately 12 inches in diameter. Roll half the circle onto the rolling pin; carefully lift the dough off floured surface, and set it on the desired size pie plate; unroll dough to cover plate (avoid stretching dough). Gently ease dough into pie plate. Trim dough to ½ inch beyond edge of pie plate. Flute edges of dough, or fold them under and press with the tines of a fork to decorate. See following instructions for specific pastry shell preparations:

UNBAKED PASTRY SHELL: Prepare pastry shell as above; set aside until ready to fill.

PARTIALLY BAKED PASTRY SHELL: Preheat oven to 450°F. Prepare shell as above, and bake for amount of time given in recipe used. Cool completely before filling.

BAKED PASTRY SHELL: Preheat oven to 450°F. Prepare crust as above. Prick unbaked shell ½ inch apart over bottom and sides with a fork. Bake for 10 to 12 minutes. Cool completely before filling.

Variation: For Nut Pastry Shell, toss ⅓ cup ground nuts with flour and salt. Prepare as directed.

Chocolate Chip Bavarian Pie

8 servings

CRUST
1 9-inch Chocolate Cookie Crumb Crust, page 184.

FILLING
1 envelope unflavored gelatin
¼ cup cold water
½ cup granulated sugar
Dash of salt
1¾ cups milk

2 egg yolks, beaten
1 teaspoon vanilla
2 egg whites, at room
*   temperature*
1 cup whipping cream
⅔ cup mini chocolate chips

GARNISH
1 tablespoon confectioners'
*   sugar, sifted*

½ cup reserved whipped cream

Prepare Chocolate Cookie Crumb Crust; set aside.

For filling, sprinkle gelatin over cold water in a cup; set aside. Mix together granulated sugar and salt in top of a double boiler. Place double boiler over simmering water; slowly stir in milk. Heat mixture until sugar dissolves. Slowly blend about ¼ cup of the hot mixture into beaten egg yolks; stir egg mixture into mixture in double boiler. Cook, stirring constantly, for about 15 minutes, or until mixture coats a metal spoon. Add softened gelatin and vanilla, stirring until gelatin dissolves. Remove from heat; pour mixture into a bowl, and cool for 15 minutes. Chill gelatin mixture until it is the consistency of unbeaten egg whites.

Beat egg whites in a small mixing bowl on high speed until stiff peaks form. Gently fold beaten egg whites into chilled mixture. Beat whipping cream in a chilled small bowl with clean, chilled beaters until stiff. Reserve ½ cup for garnish; fold remaining whipped cream into filling. Fold in mini chocolate chips. Spoon filling into prepared crust.

For garnish, stir sifted confectioners' sugar into reserved whipped cream. Garnish pie with sweetened whipped cream. Chill for at least 2 hours before serving.

Variations: For a change of pace, try any one of the following:

COCOA CHIP BAVARIAN PIE: Stir in ¼ cup unsweetened cocoa along with sugar and salt in filling.

MAPLE CHIP BAVARIAN PIE: Instead of vanilla, stir in 1½ to 2 teaspoons maple extract.

MOCHA CHIP BAVARIAN PIE: Stir in ¼ cup unsweetened cocoa and 2 teaspoons instant coffee along with sugar and salt in filling.

ORANGE CHIP BAVARIAN PIE: Instead of vanilla, stir in grated peel of 1 orange.

Coconut Chiffon Pie

---

8 servings

CRUST
1 9-inch Chocolate Coconut Crust, page 186.

FILLING
1 envelope unflavored gelatin
¼ cup cold water
1½ cups milk
3 egg yolks
¼ cup granulated sugar

1 teaspoon almond extract
3 egg whites, at room
*   temperature*
¼ cup granulated sugar
½ cup whipping cream
¾ cup flaked coconut

GARNISH
½ cup flaked coconut

½ cup mini chocolate chips

Prepare Chocolate Coconut Crust; set aside.

For filling, sprinkle gelatin over cold water in a cup; set aside. Scald milk in a small saucepan over medium-low heat. Beat egg yolks with a wire whisk in the top of a double boiler until thick and pale. Slowly stir in scalded milk. Add ¼ cup sugar. Place double boiler over simmering water, and cook, stirring constantly, until mixture coats a metal spoon. Remove from heat; add gelatin mixture and almond extract, stirring until gelatin is dissolved. Pour mixture into a bowl, and cool for 15 minutes; refrigerate, stirring occasionally, until mixture mounds when dropped from a spoon.

Beat egg whites in a small mixing bowl on high speed until foamy. Gradually add ¼ cup sugar, beating until stiff peaks form. Beat chilled gelatin mixture with a wire whisk until smooth. Gently fold in beaten egg whites. Beat whipping cream in a clean small bowl with clean beaters until stiff. Fold coconut into whipped cream. Fold whipped cream mixture into filling. Spoon filling into prepared crust.

For garnish, sprinkle pie with coconut and mini chocolate chips. Chill pie for about 2 hours, or until set.

Note: Remove Coconut Chip Chiffon Pie from the refrigerator 10 minutes before serving to soften chocolate in crust.

Grasshopper Chip Pie

8 servings

CRUST
9-inch Chocolate Cookie Crumb Crust, page 184.

FILLING

1 envelope unflavored gelatin
¼ cup granulated sugar
½ cup cold water
3 egg yolks, beaten
6 tablespoons green crème de menthe liqueur

2 tablespoons white crème de cacao liqueur
3 egg whites, at room temperature
¼ cup granulated sugar
1 cup whipping cream
⅔ cup mini chocolate chips

Prepare Chocolate Cookie Crumb Crust; set aside.

For filling, combine gelatin and ¼ cup sugar in top of a double boiler over simmering water; add water. Slowly blend in beaten egg yolks. Stir for about 5 minutes, or until gelatin dissolves and mixture thickens. Remove double boiler from water; stir in crème de menthe and crème de cacao. Pour into bowl, and refrigerate, stirring occasionally, until mixture is the consistency of unbeaten egg whites.

Beat egg whites in a small mixing bowl on high speed until foamy. Gradually add ¼ cup sugar, beating until stiff. Gently fold beaten egg whites into chilled mixture. Beat whipping cream in a chilled small bowl with clean beaters until stiff. Fold whipped cream into filling. Fold in mini chocolate chips. Spoon filling into prepared crust. Chill pie for several hours, or overnight if possible.

Variation: For Brandy Alexander Pie, substitute ¼ cup brandy and ¼ cup dark crème de cacao for crème de menthe and white crème de cacao. Make as directed.

Marbled Chocolate Rum Pie

8 servings

CRUST
1 9-inch Chocolate Nut Crumb Crust, page 184.

FILLING

1 envelope unflavored gelatin
¼ cup granulated sugar
Dash of salt
1 cup milk
2 egg yolks, beaten

2 cups semisweet chocolate
* chips*
6 tablespoons dark rum
2 egg whites, at room
* temperature*
½ cup granulated sugar

½ cup whipping cream
2 tablespoons confectioners'
* sugar*

½ teaspoon vanilla

Prepare Chocolate Nut Crumb Crust; set aside.

For filling, combine gelatin, ¼ cup granulated sugar, and salt in top of a double boiler over simmering water; add milk. Slowly blend in beaten egg yolks. Cook, stirring constantly, for about 8 minutes, or until mixture slightly thickens. Remove from heat; add chocolate chips, stirring until melted. Add rum. Pour mixture into a bowl, and cool for 15 minutes; refrigerate, stirring occasionally, until mixture is the consistency of unbeaten egg whites.

Beat egg whites in a small mixing bowl on high speed until foamy. Gradually add ½ cup granulated sugar, beating until stiff peaks form. Gently fold beaten egg whites into chilled mixture. Spoon filling into prepared crust.

Beat whipping cream, confectioners' sugar, and vanilla, in a chilled small bowl with clean, chilled beaters until stiff. Drop whipped cream by scattered tablespoonfuls onto top of filling. Using a knife, gently swirl whipped cream through filling to marbleize. Chill pie for at least 2 hours before serving.

Variation: For Chocolate Chiffon Pie, fold whipped cream into filling before spooning into prepared crust. Garnish with additional sweetened whipped cream if desired.

For best flavor and texture, eat pies when they are fresh.

Raspberry Mini Chip Chiffon Pie

8 servings

CRUST
1 *9-inch Chocolate Cookie Crumb Crust, page 184.*

FILLING
2½ *cups fresh raspberries*   ¾ *cup water*
¼ *cup granulated sugar*   2 *egg whites, at room*
1 *tablespoon lemon juice*   *temperature*
1 *envelope unflavored gelatin*   ¼ *cup granulated sugar*
¼ *cup granulated sugar*   1 *cup whipping cream*
                                     ⅔ *cup mini chocolate chips*

GARNISH
2 *tablespoons confectioners'*   1 *cup reserved whipped cream*
   sugar, sifted   *Reserved raspberries*

Prepare Chocolate Cookie Crumb Crust; set aside.

For filling, crush enough of the raspberries in a large bowl to measure 1¼ cups; set aside remaining raspberries for garnish. Stir ¼ cup granulated sugar and lemon juice into crushed raspberries; let stand for 30 minutes.

Stir together gelatin and ¼ cup granulated sugar in a small saucepan; add water. Place saucepan over medium-low heat, and stir constantly until gelatin dissolves. Remove from heat; cool. Stir cooled gelatin mixture into crushed raspberries. Chill, stirring occasionally, for about 30 minutes, or until mixture is the consistency of corn syrup.

Remove gelatin mixture from refrigerator (mixture will continue to set). Beat egg whites in a mixing bowl on high speed until foamy. Gradually add ¼ cup granulated sugar, beating until stiff peaks form. When gelatin mixture is the consistency of unbeaten egg whites, fold in beaten egg whites. Beat whipping cream in a chilled small bowl with clean, chilled beaters until stiff; reserve 1 cup for garnish. Gently fold remaining whipped cream into filling. Fold in mini chocolate chips. Spoon filling into prepared crust.

For garnish, stir sifted confectioners' sugar into 1 cup reserved whipped cream. Spoon sweetened whipped cream into a pastry bag with a rosette tip. Pipe whipped cream rosettes onto pie; top with reserved whole raspberries. Chill pie overnight.

Crème de Cacao Marshmallow Pie

8 servings

CRUST

1 9-inch Chocolate Cookie Crumb Crust, page 184.

FILLING

24 large marshmallows
½ cup milk
1⅓ cups semisweet chocolate chips

6 tablespoons crème de cacao liqueur
1½ cups whipping cream

GARNISH

2 tablespoons confectioners' sugar
1 cup reserved whipped cream

¼ cup mini chocolate chips

Prepare Chocolate Cookie Crumb Crust; set aside.

For filling, melt marshmallows with milk in a 2-quart heavy saucepan over low heat, stirring until smooth. Pour melted marshmallow mixture into a large bowl. Cool to room temperature.

Melt semisweet chocolate chips in top of a double boiler over simmering water, stirring until smooth. Remove from heat; stir in crème de cacao. Fold chocolate mixture into marshmallow mixture, blending well. Beat whipping cream in a chilled small bowl with chilled beaters until stiff; reserve 1 cup for garnish. Gently fold remaining whipped cream into chocolate mixture. Spoon filling into prepared crust.

For garnish, stir sifted confectioners' sugar into reserved whipped cream. Decorate pie with sweetened whipped cream and mini chocolate chips. Chill pie for at least 1 hour.

Variations: The following crust and liqueur combinations are only a few that can be substituted for the Chocolate Cookie Crumb Crust and crème de cacao:

Chocolate Cinnamon Crumb Crust: amaretto liqueur
Chocolate Mint Crumb Crust: crème de menthe liqueur
Chocolate Orange Crumb Crust: orange liqueur
Mocha Crumb Crust: coffee liqueur

Banana Cream Pie

8 servings

CRUST
1 9-inch Baked Pastry Shell, page 187.

PIE FILLING
3 bananas
1 tablespoon lemon juice
¾ cup granulated sugar
3 tablespoons cornstarch

2 cups milk
3 egg yolks, slightly beaten
2 tablespoons butter
1 teaspoon vanilla

MERINGUE
3 egg whites, at room
temperature
6 tablespoons granulated sugar

¼ teaspoon cream of tartar
⅓ cup mini chocolate chips

Prepare Baked Pastry Shell; set aside.

For filling, slice bananas and toss with lemon juice; drain. Arrange bananas on the bottom of cooled baked pie shell; set aside.

Combine sugar and cornstarch in a 2-quart heavy saucepan; slowly stir in milk. Place saucepan over medium heat, and cook, stirring constantly, until mixture is thick and bubbly. Continue to cook for 2 minutes. Remove from heat. Slowly blend a spoonful of hot mixture into beaten egg yolks; stir egg mixture into saucepan. Return to medium heat, and cook, stirring constantly, for 2 minutes longer. Remove from heat; stir in butter and vanilla. Pour filling over bananas in pie shell.

Preheat oven to 350°F. For meringue, beat egg whites in a small mixing bowl on high speed until foamy. Gradually add sugar and cream of tartar, beating until stiff peaks form. Fold in mini chocolate chips. Spread meringue over warm filling, spreading to edges to prevent shrinkage. Bake for 12 to 15 minutes. Cool completely. Chill until ready to serve.

When cutting a meringue-topped pie, use a wet knife to prevent sticking.

Chocolate Almond Angel Pie

8 servings

MERINGUE CRUST

4 *egg whites, at room*
  temperature
¼ *teaspoon cream of tartar*
Dash of salt

1 *cup granulated sugar*
½ *cup ground blanched*
  almonds

FILLING

1 *cup semisweet chocolate chips*
¼ *cup plus 1 tablespoon*
  amaretto liqueur

1½ *cups whipping cream*

Grease a 9-inch pie plate. Preheat oven to 300°F. For meringue crust, beat egg whites in a large mixing bowl on high speed until foamy. Add cream of tartar, salt, and sugar, and continue to beat until soft peaks form. Gently fold in ground almonds. Spread meringue onto bottom and up sides (½ inch past rim) of prepared pie plate. Bake for 50 to 55 minutes. Cool completely.

For filling, melt chocolate chips in top of a double boiler over simmering water, stirring until smooth. Remove from heat; stir in amaretto. Cool.

Beat whipping cream in a chilled mixing bowl with chilled beaters until stiff. Gently fold cool chocolate mixture into whipped cream. Spoon filling into prepared meringue shell. Chill pie for at least 2 hours.

Chocolate Cream Pie

8 to 10 servings

CRUST

1 9-inch Baked Nut Pastry Shell, page 188.

FILLING

¾ cup granulated sugar
¼ cup plus 1 tablespoon
  cornstarch
Dash of salt
2½ cups milk

½ cup semisweet chocolate
  chips
3 egg yolks, beaten
2 tablespoons butter
2 teaspoons vanilla

MERINGUE

3 egg whites, at room
  temperature
¼ teaspoon cream of tartar

6 tablespoons granulated sugar

Prepare Baked Nut Pastry Shell; set aside.

For filling, combine sugar, cornstarch, and salt in a 2-quart heavy saucepan; slowly stir in milk. Place saucepan over medium heat, and cook, stirring constantly, until mixture starts to boil. Reduce heat to low, and continue to cook, constantly stirring, for 2 minutes more. Add chocolate chips, stirring until melted. Remove from heat. Slowly blend 1 cup hot mixture into beaten egg yolks; stir egg mixture into saucepan. Return saucepan to medium heat. Bring mixture to a gentle boil, and cook for 2 minutes. Stir in butter and vanilla. Pour filling into baked pastry shell; set aside.

Preheat oven to 350°F. For meringue, beat egg whites in a mixing bowl on high speed until foamy. Add cream of tartar. Gradually add sugar, beating until stiff peaks form. Spread meringue over warm filling, spreading to edges to prevent shrinkage. Bake for 12 to 15 minutes. Cool completely. Chill pie until ready to serve.

Lemon Black Bottom Pie

8 servings

CRUST
1 9-inch Baked Pastry Shell, page 187.

FILLING

¾ cup semisweet chocolate
    chips
4 egg yolks
¼ cup lemon juice
3 tablespoons water

1 teaspoon lemon peel
½ cup granulated sugar
4 egg whites, at room
    temperature
½ cup granulated sugar

Prepare Baked Pastry Shell; set aside.

For filling, melt chocolate chips in top of a double boiler over simmering water, stirring until smooth. Spread melted chocolate over bottom of baked pie shell. Beat egg yolks in top of a double boiler with a wire whisk until thick and pale. Stir in lemon juice and water, blending well. Add lemon peel and ½ cup sugar. Place double boiler over simmering water and cook, stirring constantly for about 12 minutes or until mixture is thick. Remove from heat. Beat egg whites in a mixing bowl on high speed until foamy. Gradually add ½ cup sugar, beating until stiff peaks form. Fold half the beaten egg whites into cooked mixture; reserve the other half for topping. Pour filling over chocolate in pie shell.

Preheat oven to 325°F. Spoon remaining meringue into a pastry bag with a rosette tip. Pipe a meringue lattice over filling. Bake for 10 to 15 minutes, or until meringue is lightly browned. Cool completely. Chill until ready to serve.

Sin Pie

8 servings

CRUST
1 8-inch Chocolate Mint Crumb Crust, page 184.

FILLING
*⅔ cup semisweet chocolate
  chips
6 tablespoons butter, softened
1½ cups confectioners' sugar*

*2 eggs, beaten
1 tablespoon crème de menthe
  liqueur*

GARNISH
½ cup whipping cream

*2 tablespoons confectioners'
  sugar*

Prepare Chocolate Mint Crumb Crust; set aside.

For filling, melt chocolate chips in top of a double boiler over simmering water, stirring until smooth; remove from heat. Cream butter and confectioners' sugar in a mixing bowl on medium speed until light and fluffy (mixture should resemble whipped cream). Gradually add beaten eggs, blending well. Blend in crème de menthe and melted chocolate. Spoon filling into cooled piecrust. Chill for at least 2 hours.

For garnish, beat whipping cream and confectioners' sugar in a chilled small bowl with clean beaters until stiff. Before serving, decorate pie with whipped cream.

Chocolate Custard Pie

8 to 10 servings

CRUST
1 9-inch Unbaked Pastry Shell, page 187.

FILLING

⅔ cup semisweet chocolate
   chips
2½ cups milk
4 eggs, at room temperature

⅓ cup granulated sugar
Dash of salt
1 teaspoon vanilla

Prepare Unbaked Pastry Shell; set aside.

Preheat oven to 425°F. For filling, melt chocolate chips in top of a double boiler over simmering water, stirring until smooth. Remove from heat. Scald milk in a heavy saucepan. Gradually add scalded milk, ½ cup at a time, to melted chocolate, blending until smooth; set aside. Beat eggs, sugar, salt, and vanilla in a bowl with a rotary beater or wire whisk until smooth. Gradually pour chocolate mixture into egg mixture; blend well. Pour filling into unbaked pie shell. Bake for 15 minutes. Reduce heat to 350°F, and bake for 35 minutes longer, or until filling is set. Cool slightly. Pie may be served warm or cool. Refrigerate cooled pie.

Variation: For Chocolate Coconut Custard Pie, stir 1 cup flaked coconut and ½ cup chopped nuts into filling before pouring it into unbaked pastry shell.

To prevent custard pie filling from spilling when it is placed in the oven, pour half the filling into the pastry shell; place the pie in the oven, then carefully pour in the remaining filling, and bake.

Chocolate-Topped Custard Pie

8 servings

CRUST
1 9-inch Partially Baked Pastry Shell, page 187.

FILLING
4 eggs   *Dash of salt*
½ cup granulated sugar   *2½ cups milk*
½ teaspoon vanilla   *½ teaspoon nutmeg*

CHOCOLATE TOPPING
⅓ cup semisweet chocolate   *2 tablespoons butter*
  chips

Prepare Partially Baked Pastry Shell. Bake for 5 minutes. Cool completely before filling.

Preheat oven to 350°F. For filling, beat eggs with a wire whisk. Stir in sugar, vanilla, and salt, blending well. Stir in milk and nutmeg. Pour filling into cooled pastry shell. Place pie in oven; cover edges of pie with aluminum foil to prevent overbrowning. Bake for 30 minutes. Remove foil, and bake pie for 30 to 35 minutes longer, or until a knife inserted in center comes out clean. Cool completely.

For topping melt, chocolate chips and butter in top of a double boiler over simmering water, stirring until smooth. Drizzle topping over cooled filling with a spoon. Chill pie until ready to serve.

Variation: For the winter holidays, omit vanilla and stir in ¼ to ½ teaspoon rum or brandy extract.

Cherry Chip Royale

8 servings

TOPPING

1 16-ounce can pitted tart cherries	2 tablespoons reserved cherry juice
¼ cup granulated sugar	½ teaspoon almond extract
¼ cup cornstarch	¼ teaspoon red food coloring

CRUST

1 9-inch Ground Nut Crust, page 186.

FILLING

1 cup whipping cream	1 cup confectioners' sugar
1 8-ounce package cream cheese, softened	1 teaspoon vanilla
	½ cup mini chocolate chips

For topping, drain cherries, reserving juice. Combine granulate sugar and cornstarch in a bowl; stir in 2 tablespoons reserved cherry juice, almond extract, and red food coloring. Add cherries, stirring to coat. Let mixture stand for 1 hour.

Strain cherries, pouring liquid into a small heavy saucepan. Cook over medium-low heat, stirring constantly until mixture becomes very thick. (When the cherries are added, the mixture will thin out.) Gently fold in cherries with a rubber spatula. Cook, stirring occasionally, until mixture is once again thick. Remove from heat. Cool completely.

Prepare Ground Nut Crust. Cool completely before filling.

For filling, beat whipping cream in a chilled small bowl with chilled beaters until stiff; chill until ready to use. Beat together cream cheese and confectioners' sugar in a mixing bowl on low speed until blended. Increase speed to medium, and beat for 3 minutes. Gently fold in whipped cream and mini chocolate chips with a spoon. Spoon filling into cooled piecrust. Make a slight indentation in filling to ½ inch of edge. Spoon cooled topping into indentation. Chill until ready to serve.

Note: Canned cherry pie filling may be substituted for topping.

Chocolate Nut Ribbon Pie

8 to 10 servings

CRUST
1 9-inch Unbaked Pastry Shell, page 187.

FILLING

*1 8-ounce package cream
  cheese, softened*
⅓ cup granulated sugar

Dash of salt
1 egg
1½ teaspoons vanilla

1¼ cups nuts, chopped coarse

*½ cup semisweet chocolate
  chips*

TOPPING

*1 1-ounce square unsweetened
  chocolate*
3 eggs

¼ cup granulated sugar
1 cup light corn syrup
1 teaspoon vanilla

Prepare Unbaked Pastry Shell; set aside.

Preheat oven to 375°F. For filling, beat together cream cheese, sugar, salt, egg, and vanilla in a small mixing bowl on medium speed; blending well. Spread mixture on bottom of unbaked pastry shell. Sprinkle filling with chopped nuts and chocolate chips; set aside.

For topping, melt unsweetened chocolate in a cup set in simmering water. Remove from heat; cool. Beat eggs, sugar, corn syrup, and vanilla in a mixing bowl on medium speed until just blended. Blend in melted chocolate. Carefully pour topping over nuts and chocolate chips. Bake for 35 to 40 minutes, or until pie is set and center is firm to touch. Cool completely. Chill until ready to serve.

Crumb-Chip-Topped Cherry Pie

8 servings

CRUST
1 9-inch Unbaked Pastry Shell, page 187.

FILLING

2 16-ounce cans pitted tart cherries
¾ cup granulated sugar
⅓ cup cornstarch
Dash of salt

1 cup reserved cherry juice
¾ cup granulated sugar
¼ teaspoon almond extract
Few drops red food coloring

CRUMB CHIP TOPPING

¾ cup all-purpose flour
½ cup granulated sugar
½ cup oatmeal

½ cup nuts, chopped
½ cup butter, softened
½ cup mini chocolate chips

Prepare Unbaked Pastry Shell; set aside.

For filling, drain cherries; reserve 1 cup juice. Stir together ¾ cup sugar, cornstarch, and salt in a 2-quart heavy saucepan. Slowly stir in reserved cherry juice. Place saucepan over medium-low heat, and cook, stirring constantly, until mixture is thick and bubbly. Stir in ¾ cup sugar, cherries, almond extract, and red food coloring. Spoon filling into unbaked pie shell.

Preheat oven to 375°F. For topping, toss together flour, sugar, oatmeal, and chopped nuts in a bowl. Cut in butter with a pastry blender or two knives used scissor-fashion until mixture resembles coarse crumbs. Stir in mini chocolate chips. Sprinkle topping over filling in pie shell. Bake for 40 to 45 minutes or until topping is golden brown, and filling starts to bubble around edge. Cool completely.

Chocolate Pecan Pie

10 servings

CRUST
1 9-inch Unbaked Pastry Shell, page 187.

FILLING

¼ cup butter
1½ cups pecans
1 cup semisweet chocolate chips
½ cup light corn syrup

½ cup granulated sugar
2 eggs
1 teaspoon vanilla
1 cup pecan halves

RUM-FLAVORED WHIPPED CREAM

1 cup whipping cream
¼ cup confectioners' sugar

¼ teaspoon rum extract

Prepare Unbaked Pastry Shell; set aside.

Preheat oven to 325°F. For filling, melt butter in a small saucepan over low heat. Remove from heat; set aside. Sprinkle chopped pecans and chocolate chips over bottom of unbaked pastry shell. Beat together corn syrup, granulated sugar, eggs, and vanilla in a mixing bowl on medium speed. Add melted butter, blending well. Slowly pour mixture into unbaked pie shell. Decorate top of pie with pecan halves. Bake for 1 hour, or until firm. Cool completely.

For rum-flavored whipped cream, beat whipping cream, confectioners' sugar, and rum extract in a chilled small bowl with clean, chilled beaters until stiff. Garnish pie with whipped cream before serving.

Chocolate Brownie Pie

8 servings

CRUST
1 9-inch Unbaked Pastry Shell, page 187.

FILLING

1 14-ounce can sweetened
   condensed milk
¼ teaspoon salt
1 cup semisweet chocolate chips
1 teaspoon vanilla
2 tablespoons all-purpose flour

2 egg yolks
½ cup nuts, chopped
2 egg whites, at room
   temperature
2 tablespoons granulated sugar

Prepare Unbaked Pastry Shell; set aside.

Preheat oven to 350°F. For filling, heat sweetened condensed milk and salt in a 2-quart heavy saucepan over medium heat, stirring constantly until mixture boils. Remove from heat. Beat in chocolate chips, vanilla, and flour. Add egg yolks, one at a time, blending well after each addition. Stir in chopped nuts. Beat egg whites in a small mixing bowl on high speed until foamy. Gradually add sugar, beating until stiff peaks form. Fold whites into chocolate mixture. Pour filling into unbaked pastry shell. Bake for 40 minutes, or until firm. Cool completely.

Note: Chocolate Brownie Pie can be frozen.

Crustless Fudge Pie

8 servings

⅓ cup semisweet chocolate
   chips
½ cup butter
1 cup granulated sugar

2 eggs, beaten
¼ cup all-purpose flour
1 teaspoon vanilla
⅔ cup nuts, chopped

Grease a 9-inch pie plate; set aside. Preheat oven to 375°F. Melt chocolate chips and butter in top of a double boiler over simmering water, stirring until smooth; stir in sugar. Cool slightly. Stir in beaten eggs, flour, vanilla, and chopped nuts. Pour mixture into prepared pie plate. Bake for 25 to 30 minutes, or until set. (If edges brown too quickly, reduce heat to 350°F.) Cool slightly on wire rack. Serve pie warm or cool.

Chocolate Raisin Pie

8 servings

CRUST
1 9-inch Unbaked Pastry Shell, page 187.

FILLING
¾ cup granulated sugar
3 tablespoons cornstarch
½ teaspoon instant coffee
2 eggs, beaten
1 teaspoon vanilla

⅓ cup semisweet chocolate
* chips*
¼ cup butter
1 cup whipping cream
1½ cups raisins, chopped

GARNISH
1 cup whipping cream
¼ cup confectioners' sugar

¼ teaspoon vanilla

Prepare Unbaked Pastry Shell; set aside.

Preheat oven to 375°F. For filling, stir together granulated sugar, cornstarch, and instant coffee in a bowl. Add beaten eggs and vanilla, blending well. Set aside. Melt chocolate chips and butter with whipping cream in top of a double boiler over simmering water, stirring until smooth. Stir in chopped raisins. Slowly stir egg mixture into chocolate mixture; blend well. Pour filling into pie shell. Bake for 40 minutes, or until filling is set. Cool completely.

For garnish, beat whipping cream, confectioners' sugar, and vanilla in a chilled small bowl with chilled beaters until stiff. Chill until ready to use.

To serve, garnish each portion of pie with a dollop of whipped cream.

Note: Ungarnished pie may be kept at room temperature.

Nutty Peanut Butter Pie

8 servings

CRUST
1 9-inch Chocolate Cookie Crumb Crust, page 184.

FILLING
½ gallon vanilla ice cream,   1 cup honey
  softened   1 cup cashews, toasted and
2 cups peanut butter   chopped

CHOCOLATE FUDGE SAUCE
Chocolate Fudge Sauce, page 224.

GARNISH
1 cup whipping cream   ¼ teaspoon vanilla
2 tablespoons confectioners'
  sugar

Prepare Chocolate Cookie Crumb Crust; set aside.

For filling, mix together softened ice cream, peanut butter, honey, and chopped cashew nuts with a wooden spoon; blend well. Spoon filling into prepared crust. Freeze for at least 2 days.

Before serving, prepare Chocolate Fudge Sauce.

For garnish, beat whipping cream, confectioners' sugar, and vanilla in a chilled small mixing bowl with chilled beaters until stiff.

To serve, place pie plate in a shallow pan of warm water for 10 seconds. Top each serving with some Chocolate Fudge Sauce and a dollop of sweetened whipped cream.

Note: Chocolate Fudge Sauce may be prepared in advance, then reheated before pie is served.

Freezer Chocolate Mousse Pie

8 servings

CRUST
1 9-inch Chocolate Nut Crumb Crust, page 184.

FILLING

2 cups semisweet chocolate
   chips
1 egg
2 egg yolks

1½ teaspoons vanilla
2 egg whites, at room
   temperature
2 cups whipping cream

GARNISH

2 tablespoons confectioners'
   sugar

¼ teaspoon vanilla
1 cup reserved whipped cream

Prepare Chocolate Nut Crumb Crust; set aside.

For filling, melt chocolate chips in top of a double boiler over simmering water, stirring until smooth. Remove from heat. Beat together whole egg and egg yolks in a small bowl with a rotary beater or wire whisk. Slowly blend beaten eggs into melted chocolate chips; stir in vanilla. Beat egg whites in a small mixing bowl on high speed until stiff peaks form. Gently fold beaten egg whites into chocolate mixture. Beat whipping cream in a chilled small bowl with chilled beaters until stiff; reserve 1 cup for garnish. Fold remaining whipped cream into chocolate mixture. Spoon filling into prepared crust. Freeze for several hours.

For garnish, stir confectioners' sugar and vanilla into reserved whipped cream; chill. Before serving pie, decorate with sweetened whipped cream.

Variations: For a different flavor of filling, any one of the following may be folded in with the whipped cream:

FREEZER CHERRY CHOCOLATE MOUSSE PIE
½ cup maraschino cherries, drained and chopped

FREEZER ORANGE CHOCOLATE MOUSSE PIE
1 tablespoon grated orange peel

Freezer pies taste better if allowed to sit at room temperature for 10 to 15 minutes before serving.

Frozen Pecan Pie

---

8 servings

CRUST
1 9-inch Chocolate Nut Crumb Crust, page 184.

FILLING
4 egg yolks
¼ cup pure maple syrup
3 tablespoons corn syrup
3 egg whites, at room
   temperature

2 tablespoons granulated sugar
1 cup whipping cream
1¼ cups pecans, chopped
   coarse

TOPPING
¼ cup semisweet chocolate
   chips

1½ tablespoons butter

Prepare Chocolate Nut Crumb Crust; set aside.
For filling, beat egg yolks in top of a double boiler with a wire whisk until thick and pale. Slowly stir in maple syrup and corn syrup. Place double boiler over simmering water, and cook, stirring constantly, until mixture is thickened. Remove double boiler from hot water; place in a bowl of cold water, stirring until mixture is cool. Beat egg whites in a mixing bowl on high speed until foamy. Gradually add sugar, beating until stiff peaks form. Fold beaten egg whites into cooled mixture. Beat whipping cream in a chilled small bowl with chilled beaters until stiff. Gently fold whipped cream into filling. Fold in chopped pecans. Spoon filling into prepared crust.

For topping, melt chocolate chips and butter in a small heavy saucepan over low heat, stirring until smooth. Drizzle warm topping over filling. Cover and freeze for 8 hours, or until solid. Remove pie from freezer 15 minutes before serving.

Mocha Swirl Pie

8 servings

CRUST
1 9-inch Chocolate Cookie Crumb Crust, page 184.

FILLING

2 teaspoons instant coffee
2 tablespoons hot water
⅓ cup semisweet chocolate
  chips
1 3-ounce package cream
  cheese, softened

1 14-ounce can sweetened
  condensed milk
2 tablespoons coffee liqueur
1 cup whipping cream

CHOCOLATE TOPPING
⅓ cup semisweet chocolate chips

Prepare Chocolate Cookie Crumb Crust; set aside.

For filling, dissolve coffee in water in a small bowl; set aside. Melt chocolate chips in a measuring cup set in simmering water, stirring until smooth; set aside. Beat cream cheese in a large mixing bowl on medium speed until fluffy. Add sweetened condensed milk, coffee, coffee liqueur, and melted chocolate; blend well. Beat whipping cream in a chilled small bowl with clean, chilled beaters until stiff. Gently fold whipped cream into chocolate mixture. Cover filling, and place in freezer for 1 hour.

For topping, melt chocolate chips in top of a double boiler over simmering water, stirring until smooth. Remove from heat.

To assemble pie, pour filling into prepared crust. Spoon half of chocolate topping over filling. Swirl topping through filling with a knife to marbleize. Drizzle remaining topping over surface with a spoon. Cover pie, and freeze overnight.

Super Banana Split Pie

8 servings

CRUST
1 9-inch Chocolate Crunch Crust, page 186.

FILLING
2 bananas
1 tablespoon lemon juice

1 quart chocolate or vanilla ice cream, softened

TOPPING
½ cup whipping cream

2 tablespoons confectioners' sugar

12 maraschino cherries, drained

¼ cup nuts, chopped

Chocolate Fudge Sauce, page 224.

Prepare Chocolate Crunch Crust; chill until ready to fill.

For filling, cut bananas into thin slices, and toss with lemon juice. Arrange banana slices on the bottom of prepared crust. Carefully spread softened ice cream over bananas. Freeze pie for at least 1 hour. Remove from freezer 15 minutes before serving.

For topping, beat whipping cream with confectioners' sugar in a chilled small bowl with chilled beaters until stiff. Spread whipped cream over frozen pie; for garnish, top whipped cream with maraschino cherries and chopped nuts.

To serve, drizzle pie with warm Chocolate Fudge Sauce. Serve immediately.

Raspberry Swirl Pie

8 servings

CRUST

1 9-inch Graham Cracker
Crumb Crust, page 185.

¾ cup mini chocolate chips

FILLING

1 quart raspberry sherbet

1 pint vanilla ice cream

Preheat oven to 350°F. Prepare Graham Cracker Crumb Crust. Sprinkle chocolate chips over bottom of crust. Bake for 10 minutes, or until chocolate chips begin to melt and crust is golden. Cool completely before filling.

For filling, have raspberry sherbet and vanilla ice cream at room temperature to soften slightly. Place sherbet in a large bowl. Fold in ice cream with a spoon to marbleize. Spoon filling into cooled crust. Cover and freeze for at least 2 hours or overnight if possible. Remove pie from freezer 15 minutes before serving.

Chocolate Chip
Beverages, Ice Cream,
and Sauces

This chapter is a mixture of recipes devoted to beverages, ice creams, and sauces, all made with chocolate chips. Sit back and enjoy a cup of hot chocolate or cappuccino, made thick and rich with melted chips, which will render the chocoholic almost senseless with delight. A trip to the ice cream parlor is only pages away. There may be found a variety of frosty and tempting recipes loaded with chocolate chips. Dress up a dessert with a cascade of melted chocolate chip sauce—plain, nutty, or spiked with a favorite liqueur. Chocolate chips are in abundant portions throughout this chapter.

Hot Chocolate

4 servings

¾ cup semisweet chocolate   4 cups milk
   chips

Melt chocolate chips with milk in a 2-quart heavy saucepan over low heat, stirring until smooth. Pour into mugs.

Variations: Any one of the following may be added to hot chocolate:

ALMOND HOT CHOCOLATE
   ½ teaspoon almond extract

ALMOND MOCHA CHOCOLATE
   1½ teaspoons instant coffee
   ¼ teaspoon almond extract

CANADIAN HOT CHOCOLATE
   ½ teaspoon maple extract

CHERRY-FLAVORED HOT CHOCOLATE
   ½ teaspoon cherry extract or 2 tablespoons maraschino cherry
      juice

MINTY HOT CHOCOLATE
   ¼ teaspoon mint extract

ORANGE HOT CHOCOLATE
   ½ teaspoon orange extract

SWISS MOCHA HOT CHOCOLATE
   1½ teaspoons instant coffee
   1 teaspoon vanilla

VIENNESE HOT CHOCOLATE
¼ *teaspoon cinnamon*
¼ *teaspoon nutmeg*
1 *teaspoon vanilla*

French Chocolate

---

6 servings

½ *cup semisweet chocolate* *chips*	1 *teaspoon vanilla* 1 *cup whipping cream*
¼ *cup light corn syrup*	4 *cups milk*
¼ *cup hot water*	

Melt chocolate chips with corn syrup and hot water in a small heavy saucepan over low heat, stirring until smooth. Add vanilla. Remove from heat, and cool to room temperature. Chill.

Beat whipping cream in a chilled small mixing bowl with chilled beaters until stiff. Gradually add chilled chocolate, beating until mixture mounds when dropped from a spoon. Chill.

Just before serving, heat milk (do not boil). Fill six mugs half-full with chilled mixture. Fill with warm milk; stir to blend.

Mexican Hot Chocolate

---

6 servings

4 *cups milk*	1 *teaspoon cinnamon*
½ *cup semisweet chocolate* *chips*	2 *eggs* 6 *3-inch sticks cinnamon*

Scald milk in a 3-quart heavy saucepan over medium heat. Add chocolate chips and cinnamon, stirring until chocolate is melted. Beat mixture with a rotary beater until smooth. Remove from heat. Beat eggs in a small bowl. Slowly beat 1 cup of the hot mixture into eggs. Stir egg mixture back into hot mixture in pan. Return pan to heat. Cook, stirring constantly, for 1 minute. Beat mixture with a rotary beater until frothy. Serve Mexican Hot Chocolate in mugs garnished with cinnamon sticks.

Mocha Cream

6 servings

1 cup semisweet chocolate chips
1 cup boiling water
¼ cup granulated sugar

5 cups milk
2 tablespoons instant coffee
2 teaspoons vanilla
6 large marshmallows

Melt chocolate chips with boiling water and sugar in top of a double boiler over simmering water, stirring until smooth. Remove from heat. Combine milk, instant coffee, and vanilla in a large saucepan over medium heat. Heat until mixture begins to simmer. Gradually add chocolate mixture to milk, beating with a wire whisk. Serve Mocha Cream garnished with marshmallows.

Three Schnapps to the Wind

6 servings

1 cup semisweet chocolate chips
¾ cup water
2½ cups milk

1 cup whipping cream
3 tablespoons peppermint
    schnapps

Melt chocolate chips with water in a 2-quart heavy saucepan over low heat, stirring until smooth. Slowly stir in milk and cream, blending well; heat thoroughly. Remove from heat, and stir in peppermint schnapps. Pour into mugs.

Variation: Any one of the following may be substituted for peppermint schnapps:

Brandy   *Raspberry liqueur*
Coffee liqueur   *Rum*
Crème de cacao liqueur   *Orange liqueur*
Crème de menthe liqueur

Orange Cappuccino

---

4 servings

½ cup semisweet chocolate chips   *1½ teaspoons granulated sugar (optional)*
2 cups milk   *2 cups hot strong coffee*
                                           ½ cup orange liqueur

Melt chocolate chips with milk and sugar in a 2-quart heavy saucepan over low heat, stirring until smooth. Fill four large mugs half-full with chocolate mixture; pour in enough hot coffee almost to fill. Add 2 tablespoons orange liqueur to each mug.

Variation: For Café Mexicano, add 2 tablespoons sugar to chocolate mixture, along with 1½ teaspoons vanilla and ½ teaspoon cinnamon, in a blender, and blend for 1 minute. Fill four large mugs half-full with chocolate mixture; pour in enough coffee almost to fill. Instead of orange liqueur, add 2 tablespoons brandy to each mug. Garnish each mug with a cinnamon stick.

Banana Split Ice Cream

Makes about 1½ quarts

1¼ cups granulated sugar
1 cup light cream
1 teaspoon vanilla
¼ cup lemon juice
½ cup sour cream
1½ cups mashed bananas

2 cups whipping cream
1 tablespoon almond liqueur
½ cup nuts, chopped coarse
½ cup maraschino cherries,
    drained and chopped
½ cup mini chocolate chips

Combine sugar and light cream in top of a double boiler over simmering water. Cook, stirring constantly, until sugar is dissolved. Remove from heat; add vanilla. Cool to room temperature.

Stir together lemon juice, sour cream, and mashed bananas in a large bowl. Add cooled sugar mixture and whipping cream. Stir in almond liqueur. Transfer mixture into ice cream canister. Prepare ice cream according to freezer's directions.

When ice cream is frozen, stir in chopped nuts, chopped maraschino cherries, and mini chocolate chips.

Chocolate Peanut Butter Ice Cream

Makes about 2 quarts

1 cup semisweet chocolate chips
2 cups milk
1 cup granulated sugar

½ cup peanut butter
2 cups whipping cream
1½ teaspoons vanilla

Melt chocolate chips with milk and sugar in a 3-quart heavy saucepan over low heat, stirring until smooth. Blend in peanut butter. Remove from heat; cool to room temperature. Stir in whipping cream and vanilla. Transfer mixture into ice cream canister. Prepare ice cream according to freezer's directions.

Chocolate Ripple Ice Cream

Makes about 2 quarts

1½ cups granulated sugar
¼ cup all-purpose flour
¼ teaspoon salt
2 cups milk

4 eggs, beaten
4 cups whipping cream
2 tablespoons vanilla

CHOCOLATE SAUCE
1 cup semisweet chocolate chips
2 tablespoons butter

¼ cup light corn syrup
2 tablespoons hot water

Combine sugar, flour, salt, and milk in a 3-quart heavy saucepan over medium heat. Cook, stirring constantly, for about 2 minutes, or until mixture thickens and bubbles. Slowly blend half the hot mixture into eggs. Stir egg mixture into the mixture in saucepan. Cook, stirring constantly, for 1 minute. Pour mixture into a large bowl; stir in whipping cream and vanilla. Chill for at least 2 hours.

Prepare chocolate sauce 1 hour before freezing ice cream. Melt chocolate chips and butter with corn syrup and hot water in top of a double boiler over simmering water, stirring until smooth. Remove from heat; cool (do not chill).

Transfer cream mixture in ice cream canister. Prepare according to freezer's directions.

When ice cream is frozen, lightly fold in chocolate sauce for a rippled effect.

Cocoa Chip Ice Cream

Makes about 2 quarts

1 cup granulated sugar
6 tablespoons unsweetened
   cocoa
2 cups whipping cream

2 cups light cream
2 teaspoons vanilla
1 cup mini chocolate chips

Stir together sugar and cocoa in a bowl. Pour whipping cream and light cream into ice cream canister. Add cocoa mixture, stirring until sugar is dissolved. Add vanilla. Prepare ice cream according to freezer's directions.

When ice cream is frozen, stir in mini chocolate chips.

Mocha Ice Cream

Makes about 1 gallon

2 cups semisweet chocolate chips	1⅔ cups granulated sugar
¼ cup instant coffee crystals	¼ teaspoon salt
2 cups light cream	6 cups light cream
	3 tablespoons vanilla

Melt chocolate chips with instant coffee in top of a double boiler over simmering water, stirring until smooth. Remove from heat. Scald 2 cups light cream in a 2-quart heavy saucepan over medium heat; remove from heat. Add sugar and salt, stirring until dissolved. Transfer mixture into ice cream canister; stir in chocolate mixture, blending well. Pour in 6 cups light cream. Chill thoroughly.

Just before freezing, stir in vanilla. Prepare ice cream according to freezer's directions.

Variation: For Almond Mocha Ice Cream, stir 1½ cups chopped toasted almonds into frozen ice cream.

Real Rocky Road Ice Cream

Makes about 1 gallon

4 1-ounce squares unsweetened chocolate	4 cups whipping cream
2 cups milk	2 tablespoons vanilla
1¾ cups granulated sugar	2 cups mini marshmallows
¼ teaspoon salt	1 cup walnuts, chopped
2 cups milk	1 cup semisweet chocolate chips

Melt unsweetened chocolate in top of a double boiler over simmering water, stirring until smooth; set aside. Scald 2 cups milk in a 2-quart heavy saucepan over medium heat; remove from heat. Add sugar and salt, stirring until dissolved. Stir in melted chocolate. (If mixture becomes grainy, use an electric blender until smooth.) Add 2 cups milk. Transfer chocolate mixture in a bowl. Chill thoroughly.

Just before freezing, pour whipping cream and vanilla into ice cream canister. Prepare ice cream according to freezer's directions.

When ice cream is frozen, stir in mini marshmallows, chopped walnuts, and chocolate chips.

Rum Raisin Chip Ice Cream

Makes about 1 gallon

2 cups dark raisins, chopped	*2 cups milk*
⅓ cup dark rum	*4 cups whipping cream*
2 cups milk	*2 tablespoons vanilla*
1¾ cups granulated sugar	*1 cup pecans, chopped coarse*
¾ teaspoon salt	*1 cup mini chocolate chips*

Soak chopped raisins in rum in a bowl for several hours or overnight if possible.

Scald 2 cups milk in a 2-quart heavy saucepan over medium heat; remove from heat. Add sugar and salt, stirring until dissolved. Add 2 cups milk. Transfer mixture into a bowl. Chill thoroughly.

Just before freezing, pour whipping cream and vanilla into ice cream canister. Prepare ice cream according to freezer's directions.

When ice cream is frozen, stir in raisin and rum mixture, chopped pecans, and mini chocolate chips.

Vanilla Chip Ice Cream

Makes about 2 quarts

2 eggs	*2 cups whipping cream*
1 cup granulated sugar	*1 tablespoon vanilla*
2 cups milk	*1 cup mini chocolate chips*

Beat eggs in a large bowl with a wire whisk until thick and pale. Beat in sugar until light and fluffy. (An electric mixer may be used.) Stir in milk, whipping cream, and vanilla, blending well. Transfer mixture into ice cream canister. Prepare according to freezer's directions.

When ice cream is frozen, stir in mini chocolate chips.

Variations: This versatile ice cream's flavor may be changed by adding any one of the following:

COFFEE CHIP ICE CREAM: Add 4 teaspoons instant coffee to ice cream mixture before freezing.

GRANOLA CHIP ICE CREAM: Decrease amount of mini chocolate chips to ½ cup, and add 1½ cups granola.

MINT CHIP ICE CREAM: Add ½ to ¾ teaspoon mint extract and a few drops green food coloring to ice cream mixture before freezing.

Chocolate Sauce

Makes about 1½ cups

¼ cup light corn syrup	*2 tablespoons butter*
2 tablespoons hot water	*1 cup semisweet chocolate chips*

Combine corn syrup, hot water, and butter in a heavy saucepan over medium-low heat; bring to a boil. Remove from heat; stir in chocolate chips, blending until melted. Cool slightly.

Chocolate Caramel Sauce

Makes about 1 cup

²/₃ cup semisweet chocolate
   chips
1 cup brown sugar, packed
   firm

½ cup whipping cream
1 tablespoon butter
1 teaspoon vanilla

Melt chocolate chips in top of a double boiler over simmering water, stirring until smooth. Add brown sugar, whipping cream, and butter, blending well. Cook until mixture is smooth and thick. Remove from heat; stir in vanilla. Serve warm.

Chocolate Fudge Sauce

Makes about 1 cup

⅓ cup semisweet chocolate
   chips
½ cup sweetened condensed
   milk

¼ cup water
2 tablespoons butter

Melt chocolate chips with sweetened condensed milk in top of a double boiler over simmering water, stirring until smooth. Beat in water and butter. Serve sauce hot.

Easy Fudge Walnut Sauce

Makes about 2 cups

2 cups semisweet chocolate   1 cup butter
  chips   1 cup walnuts, chopped coarse

Melt chocolate chips and butter in top of a double boiler over simmering water, stirring until smooth. Stir in chopped walnuts. Serve sauce warm.

Note: Leftover Easy Fudge Walnut Sauce may be refrigerated. To reheat, place container in which it has been stored in a saucepan filled with water. Warm over low heat until sauce is pouring consistency.

Chocolate Flambé Sauce

Makes 1¾ cups

1 cup semisweet chocolate chips   ¼ cup light corn syrup
1 tablespoon butter   ¼ cup milk
                                  ¼ cup liqueur

Melt chocolate chips and butter with light corn syrup and milk in top of a double boiler over simmering water, stirring until smooth. Warm liqueur in a saucepan; ignite. Carefully pour flaming liqueur into chocolate mixture. When flame subsides, stir to blend. Spoon sauce over ice cream.

Chocolate Rum Sauce

Makes about 2 cups

1 cup semisweet chocolate chips   *⅔ cup whipping cream*
                                     ½ cup dark rum

Melt chocolate chips in top of a double boiler over simmering water, stirring until smooth. Stir in whipping cream and rum; blend well. Sauce may be served warm or cool.

Note: Brandy or different flavors of liqueur may be substituted for rum in this recipe.

Chocolate Banana Sauce

Makes about 2 cups

1 cup semisweet chocolate chips   *⅓ cup whipping cream*
1 tablespoon butter   *3 tablespoons dark rum*
                                     2 bananas

Melt chocolate chips and butter with whipping cream and rum in top of a double boiler over simmering water, stirring until smooth. Slice bananas into chocolate mixture; lightly stir to coat. Serve sauce warm.

We Wish You
a Merry Chipmas

'Tis the season of goodwill, and there is no better way to promote it than with chocolate chips. They add an extra-special touch to traditional Christmas fare. On the following pages, chocolate chips are paired with customary holiday foods, such as candied fruits, eggnog, and marzipan, to bring about new delights. They make novel and exciting treats out of Old World yeast breads, and add a satisfying taste of chocolate to yuletide candies and cookies. These recipes are great for family get-togethers or gift giving, guaranteed to leave everyone with "visions of chocolate chips dancing through their heads!"

Almond Chip Wreath

---

1 coffee cake

DOUGH
¾ cup milk
1 package active dry yeast
¼ cup warm (105° to 115°)
 water
⅓ cup granulated sugar

⅓ cup butter, softened
½ teaspoon salt
1 egg, at room temperature
3½ to 4 cups all-purpose or
 bread flour

CHOCOLATE ALMOND FILLING
½ cup almond paste
¼ cup brown sugar, packed
 firm

¼ cup butter, softened
¾ cup mini chocolate chips

GLAZE
1 cup confectioners' sugar
1 tablespoon milk

½ teaspoon vanilla

GARNISH (optional)
Maraschino cherry halves, walnut halves, semisweet chocolate
 chips

Grease a large bowl; set aside. Scald milk in a heavy saucepan; cool. Dissolve yeast in warm water in a large mixing bowl. Stir in cooled milk, granulated sugar, softened butter, salt, egg, and 2 cups flour. Beat on medium speed until smooth. Mix in enough remaining flour, 1 cup at a time, to make dough soft and easy to handle. Turn dough onto lightly floured surface; knead for about 5 minutes, or until smooth and elastic. Place dough in prepared bowl; turn greased side up. Cover and let rise in a warm, draft-free place until double, about 1½ hours, or when indentation remains when lightly touched.

Meanwhile, for chocolate almond filling, mix together almond paste, brown sugar, and softened butter until smooth; set aside.

Roll dough on a lightly floured surface into a 15 × 9-inch rectangle. Spread filling evenly over dough. Sprinkle mini chocolate chips over filling. Starting with larger edge, roll dough up tightly. Pinch edge of dough into roll to seal well. Stretch roll to make even. Pinch edges together to form a ring. Using scissors, make cuts two-thirds of the way through ring at 1-inch intervals. Carefully transfer ring to a large cookie sheet. Turn each section on its side to give ring a fanned appearance. Cover ring, and let rise in a warm, draft-free place until double, about 40 to 50 minutes. Preheat oven to 350°F. Bake for 25 to 30 minutes, or until golden brown. Cool on wire rack.

For glaze, blend confectioners' sugar, milk, and vanilla in a small mixing bowl on medium speed until smooth. Spread glaze over warm Almond Chip Wreath.

Garnish with maraschino cherries, walnut halves, or semisweet chocolate chips if desired.

Candy Cane Bread

---

2 loaves

DOUGH

1 package active dry yeast
1 teaspoon granulated sugar
¼ cup warm (105° to 115°F) water
⅓ cup granulated sugar
2 eggs, at room temperature
⅓ cup butter, melted

½ cup sour cream, at room temperature
1 teaspoon vanilla
½ teaspoon salt
3¼ to 3¾ cups all-purpose or bread flour

FILLING

¾ cup peppermint candy, crushed coarse

½ cup semisweet chocolate chips

RED EGG GLAZE

1 egg white
2 to 6 drops red food coloring

Coarse red decorating sugar (optional)

PEPPERMINT GLAZE

1 cup confectioners' sugar	*1 to 2 tablespoons milk*
1 to 2 drops peppermint extract	

GARNISH

⅓ to ½ cup peppermint candy, crushed fine

Grease a large bowl; set aside. Dissolve yeast and 1 teaspoon granulated sugar in water in a large mixing bowl. Let stand for about 5 to 10 minutes, or until foamy. Add ⅓ cup granulated sugar, eggs, melted butter, sour cream, vanilla, salt, and 1½ to 2 cups flour. Beat at medium speed with electric mixer for 2 minutes. Stir in enough remaining flour to make a soft dough. Turn dough onto slightly floured surface. Knead dough for about 4 to 6 minutes, or until soft, smooth, and not sticky. Place dough in greased bowl; turn once to coat top. Cover and let rise in a warm, draft-free place until double, about 1½ hours.

Grease two cookie sheets; set aside. Punch down dough; knead for 30 seconds. Roll dough into a 15 × 9-inch rectangle on a lightly floured surface. Sprinkle with filling of peppermint candy and chocolate chips. Fold dough over filling, then knead to distribute evenly. (Work quickly to avoid melting candy.) Divide dough into four equal pieces. Shape each piece into a 22-inch rope. Tightly twist two ropes together; pinch edges to seal. Repeat with remaining two ropes. Place twisted ropes on prepared cookie sheets, curving like candy canes. Cover and let rise in a warm, draft-free place until double, about 1 hour.

Preheat oven to 350°F. For egg glaze, mix egg white and red food coloring in a small bowl. Carefully brush every other section of twist with red egg white mixture. If desired, sprinkle red sugar over red sections of twists. Bake for 25 to 30 minutes, or until bread sounds hollow when tapped on top. Cool on wire racks.

For peppermint glaze, combine confectioners' sugar and peppermint extract in a small mixing bowl on medium speed. Stir in enough milk to make a smooth, creamy glaze of drizzling consistency. Drizzle glaze over white sections of twists. Garnish by sprinkling crushed peppermint candy over glaze.

German Stollen with Chocolate Chips

---

1 loaf

½ cup candied fruits and peels
½ cup golden raisins
2 tablespoons dark rum
⅔ cup milk
½ cup butter
¼ cup granulated sugar
1 package active dry yeast
¼ cup warm (105° to 115°F)
  water
1 egg, beaten

½ teaspoon almond extract
3¾ cups all-purpose flour
Grated peel of 1 orange
¾ cup blanched almonds,
  slivered
½ cup semisweet chocolate
  chips
¼ cup butter, melted
1 tablespoon granulated sugar
Confectioners' sugar, sifted

Grease a large bowl; set aside. Toss candied fruits and peels and raisins with rum in a bowl; let stand for several hours or overnight if possible.

Scald milk in a 2-quart heavy saucepan over medium heat; remove from heat. Add butter and ¼ cup granulated sugar, stirring until sugar is dissolved. Cool to room temperature. Dissolve yeast in warm water in a large mixing bowl. Beat in milk mixture, egg, almond extract, and 2 cups flour on low speed until blended. Increase speed to medium, and beat for 2 minutes, or until smooth. Stir in fruit mixture, orange peel, slivered almonds, and chocolate chips with a spoon. Stir in remaining flour, blending well. Turn dough out onto a lightly floured surface, and knead for about 5 minutes, or until smooth and elastic. Shape dough in a ball, and place in prepared bowl; turn once to grease top. Cover and place in a warm, draft-free place until double, about 1½ hours.

Grease a cookie sheet. Punch down dough. Roll dough out to an oval, 1 inch thick, on a lightly floured surface. Brush top with some melted butter; sprinkle with 1 tablespoon granulated sugar. Fold long side of oval over to within ½ inch, and press together. Brush with melted butter. Cover and let rise in a warm, draft-free place until double, about 1 hour.

Preheat oven to 350°F. Bake for 30 minutes, until stollen sounds hollow when tapped. Immediately upon removing from oven, brush stollen with melted butter; sprinkle with sifted confectioners' sugar. Cool.

Kugelhopf with Chocolate Chips

---

12 servings

¾ cup golden raisins
2 tablespoons dark rum
¾ cup milk
1 package active dry yeast
¼ cup warm (105° to 115°F) water
1 cup all-purpose flour
⅓ cup blanched almonds, chopped

1 cup butter, softened
¾ cup granulated sugar
5 eggs, at room temperature
3 cups all-purpose flour
Grated peel of 1 lemon
½ cup blanched almonds, chopped
¾ cup semisweet chocolate chips

Soak raisins in rum in a bowl overnight.

Scald milk in a small saucepan over medium-low heat. Remove from heat; cool to room temperature. Sprinkle yeast over warm water in a bowl; let stand for a few minutes; then stir to dissolve. Add scalded milk and 1 cup flour, stirring to blend. Cover and let rise in a warm, draft-free place until frothy, about 1½ to 2 hours.

Grease a 12-cup fluted tube pan; sprinkle bottom with ⅓ cup chopped almonds. Drain raisins. Cream butter and sugar in a large mixing bowl on medium speed until light and fluffy. Add eggs, one at a time, blending well after each addition. Blend in yeast mixture. Lower speed, and add 1 cup flour, blending well. By hand, stir in remaining flour. Stir in drained raisins, lemon peel, ½ cup chopped almonds, and chocolate chips. Pour batter into pan. Cover and let rise in a warm, draft-free place until light, about 1 to 1½ hours.

Preheat oven to 350°F. Bake for 1 hour, or until cake tester inserted in center comes out clean. Cool in pan for 5 minutes; then turn out onto a wire rack. Cool completely.

Scandinavian Julekage

1 loaf

¾ cup milk
1 package active dry yeast
¼ cup warm (105° to 115°F)
    water
¼ cup granulated sugar
Dash of salt
¼ cup butter
1 egg, at room temperature

¾ teaspoon cardamom
3½ cups all-purpose flour
⅓ cup candied fruits, chopped
⅓ cup raisins
⅓ cup semisweet chocolate
    chips
2 tablespoons butter, melted

GLAZE
1 cup confectioners' sugar
4 teaspoons water

¼ teaspoon vanilla

Grease a large bowl; set aside. Scald milk in a 2-quart heavy saucepan on medium heat. Remove from heat; cool to room temperature. Dissolve yeast in warm water in a large mixing bowl. Beat in granulated sugar, salt, ¼ cup butter, egg, cardamom, and 2 cups flour on low speed, blending well. Increase speed to medium, and beat for 2 minutes. Stir in chopped candied fruits, raisins, and chocolate chips with a spoon. Stir in remaining flour. Turn dough out onto a floured surface, and knead for about 5 minutes, or until smooth and elastic. Shape dough into ball, and place in prepared bowl; turn once to grease top. Cover and let rise in a warm, draft-free place until double, about 1½ hours.

Grease a 9-inch springform pan. Punch dough down. Shape into a ball, and place in prepared pan. Brush top with half the melted butter. Cover and let rise in a warm, draft-free place until double, about 1 hour.

Preheat oven to 350°F. Bake for 35 to 45 minutes or until cake tester inserted in center comes out clean.

Meanwhile, for glaze, beat together confectioners' sugar, water, and vanilla in a bowl until smooth. Immediately upon removing julekage from oven, remove from pan. Brush with remaining melted butter; spread with glaze. Cool.

Three Kings Bread

---

1 loaf

½ cup plus 2 tablespoons milk
1 cup granulated sugar
¼ cup butter, cut into pieces
½ teaspoon salt
1 package active dry yeast
1 egg, at room temperature

2¾ to 3 cups all-purpose flour
¼ cup raisins or currants
¼ cup diced mixed candied fruits and peels
¼ cup nuts, chopped
½ cup semisweet chocolate chips

FROSTING
1½ cups confectioners' sugar, sifted

¼ teaspoon vanilla extract
1½ to 2 tablespoons milk

GARNISH
One or more of:
candied cherries, candied pineapple, walnut halves, or chocolate chips

Grease a large mixing bowl; set aside. Heat milk, granulated sugar, butter, and salt in a heavy saucepan until warm (105° to 115°F) and butter is almost melted; stir constantly with a wooden spoon. Pour warm milk mixture into a large mixing bowl. Sprinkle in yeast, and stir until dissolved. Beat egg in a separate bowl. Add beaten egg and 1 cup flour to yeast mixture. Using an electric mixer, beat at low speed for ½ minute, scraping bowl constantly. Beat at high speed for about 3 minutes, or until mixture is smooth. By hand, stir in raisins, diced candied fruits and peels, chopped nuts, and chocolate chips. Stir in enough additional flour to make a soft dough. Turn out onto a lightly floured surface. Knead in enough flour to make a moderately stiff dough that is smooth and elastic, about 5 to 10 minutes. Shape dough into a ball. Place dough in prepared bowl; turn once to grease top. Cover and let rise in a warm, draft-free place until double, about 1½ to 2 hours.

Punch down dough. Cover and let rest for 10 minutes. Meanwhile, grease a 10-inch tube pan; set aside. Shape dough into a roll about 18 to 20 inches long. Join ends of roll together to form a ring. Place ring in prepared pan. Cover and let rise in a warm, draft-free place until almost double, about 1 hour.

Preheat oven to 350°F. Bake for 25 to 30 minutes, or until golden brown. Turn onto wire rack; invert and cool.

For frosting, combine sifted confectioners' sugar, vanilla, and 1½ tablespoons milk. Add more milk if necessary to make an icing of drizzling consistency. Drizzle frosting over cooled bread.

Garnish with candied fruit, walnut halves, or chocolate chips.

Eggnog Chip Fudge

64 pieces

2 3-ounce packages cream
   cheese, softened
½ cup dry instant eggnog
4¾ cups confectioners' sugar,
   sifted

½ cup nuts, chopped
½ cup mini chocolate chips

Line an 8-inch square pan with aluminum foil; set aside. Beat cream cheese in a small mixing bowl on medium speed until smooth. Lower speed, and add instant eggnog and sifted confectioners' sugar, blending well. Stir in chopped nuts and mini chocolate chips with a spoon. Spread mixture in prepared pan. Chill until firm. Remove from pan, and peel away foil. Cut into 1-inch squares. Store fudge in refrigerator for up to 2 weeks.

Noel Almond Crisps

Makes about 2 dozen

⅔ cup raisins
2 tablespoons dark rum
1¼ cups toasted almonds,
  chopped

3 tablespoons candied lemon
  peel, chopped fine
2 cups semisweet chocolate
  chips

Combine raisins and rum in a small bowl. Cover and soak overnight.

Cover a cookie sheet with wax paper. Toss together chopped almonds, candied lemon peel, and raisin mixture in a bowl; set aside. Melt chocolate chips in top of a double boiler over simmering water, stirring until smooth. Remove from heat. Pour melted chocolate over mixture in bowl, stirring to coat. Drop mixture by teaspoonfuls onto prepared cookie sheet. Let dry slightly; then chill until firm. Store candy in an airtight container in refrigerator.

Variation: Substitute candied orange peel for lemon peel, if desired.

Chocolate Chestnut Truffles

Makes about 2 dozen

1 cup semisweet chocolate chips
1 16-ounce can shelled whole
  chestnuts (or marrons), or
  1¼ pounds fresh chestnuts

6 tablespoons butter, softened
½ cup granulated sugar
2½ tablespoons brandy
1 teaspoon vanilla

CHOCOLATE COATING
2 cups semisweet chocolate
  chips

1 cup unsweetened cocoa, sifted
24 1-inch paper candy cups

Melt chocolate chips in top of a double boiler over simmering water, stirring until smooth. Remove from heat. Mash chestnuts in a bowl with a fork until smooth. Add butter, sugar, brandy, and vanilla; blend well. Stir in melted chocolate. Refrigerate mixture until it is firm enough to handle.

For chocolate coating, melt chocolate chips in top of a double boiler over simmering water, stirring until smooth. Remove from heat. Pour melted chocolate onto a clean plate. Allow chocolate to cool, but not to set.

To assemble truffles, roll chestnut mixture into 1-inch balls (return chestnut mixture to refrigerator if it becomes too soft to shape). Carefully roll each truffle in melted chocolate chips. Let dry briefly; then roll in sifted cocoa. Place finished truffles in paper candy cups. Store truffles in refrigerator.

Note: To prepare fresh chestnuts, use a sharp knife to cut a cross on the flat side of each chestnut shell. Put chestnuts in a large pan, and cover them with cold water. Bring water to a boil; boil for 5 minutes. Cool chestnuts until able to handle. Remove shells and inner skins.

Chocolate-Covered Marzipan

Makes about 3½ dozen

MARZIPAN

1 8-ounce can almond paste

1 egg white, at room temperature

2 cups confectioners' sugar

CHOCOLATE GLAZE

¾ cup semisweet chocolate chips

1 1-ounce square unsweetened chocolate

2 tablespoons butter

Cover a cookie sheet with wax paper; set aside. For marzipan, mash almond paste in a bowl with a fork. Beat egg white in a small mixing bowl on high speed until soft peaks form. Stir beaten egg white into almond paste. Stir in 1½ cups confectioners' sugar, blending well. On a surface dusted with remaining confectioners' sugar, knead marzipan until smooth and firm. (Add more confectioners' sugar if necessary.) Shape into ¾-inch balls. Place marzipan on prepared cookie sheet. Cover with a clean dish towel, and let stand for 1 hour.

Cover another cookie sheet with wax paper. For chocolate glaze, melt chocolates and butter in top of a double boiler over simmering water, stirring until smooth. Keep glaze warm. Dip marzipan into chocolate with a fork, coating completely. Set marzipan on prepared cookie sheet. Allow chocolate to set. Store in an airtight container with wax paper between layers of marzipan.

Note: Chocolate-Covered Marzipan may be flavored by adding ½ to ¾ teaspoon extract to it while kneading. It may also be tinted.

Chocolate Rum Balls

Makes about 4 dozen

*2½ cups chocolate cookie
    crumbs
1 cup nuts, chopped fine
½ cup confectioners' sugar,
    sifted
1 cup semisweet chocolate chips*

*2 tablespoons light corn syrup
⅓ cup dark rum
½ cup confectioners' sugar,
    sifted
2 tablespoons unsweetened
    cocoa*

Mix together chocolate cookie crumbs, chopped nuts, and ½ cup sifted confectioners' sugar in a bowl; set aside. Melt chocolate chips with corn syrup in top of a double boiler over simmering water, stirring until smooth. Remove from heat; stir in rum. Pour chocolate mixture over dry ingredients, mixing well. Stir together ½ cup sifted confectioners' sugar and cocoa in a small bowl. Shape chocolate mixture into 1-inch balls; roll in cocoa mixture. Store candy in an airtight container for 2 weeks to develop flavor.

Note: Brandy may be substituted for rum in this recipe if desired.

Pink Peppermint Brownies

Makes about 3 dozen

2 cups semisweet chocolate
    chips
⅔ cup butter
4 eggs
1 cup granulated sugar

1 teaspoon vanilla
½ cup all-purpose flour, sifted
1 teaspoon baking powder
½ cup nuts, chopped

TOPPING

3 cups confectioners' sugar
½ cup peppermint candy,
    crushed

1 3-ounce package cream
    cheese, softened
¼ cup butter, softened
6 to 8 tablespoons milk

Peppermint candy (optional)

Grease a 13 × 9 × 2-inch pan; set aside. Preheat oven to 350°F. Melt chocolate chips and butter in top of a double boiler over simmering water, stirring until smooth; set aside. Beat together eggs and granulated sugar in a mixing bowl on medium speed. Add vanilla. Blend in melted chocolate mixture. Lower speed, and add sifted flour and baking powder, blending well. Stir in chopped nuts with a spoon. Pour batter into prepared pan. Bake for 25 minutes. Cool completely.

For topping, beat confectioners' sugar, crushed peppermint candy, cream cheese, butter, and milk in a medium mixing bowl on medium speed until light and fluffy. Spread topping over cooled brownies. Cut into bars. Top each bar with additional peppermint candy if desired.

Eggnog Chip Bars

Makes 4 dozen

¾ cup butter, softened
1½ cups granulated sugar
2 eggs, at room temperature
½ teaspoon brandy extract
½ teaspoon rum extract
¼ cup dairy eggnog

1/4 teaspoon nutmeg
¼ teaspoon cinnamon
1 teaspoon baking soda
2¾ cups all-purpose flour
1 cup semisweet chocolate chips

TOPPING
2 tablespoons granulated sugar

2 tablespoons red or green colored sugar

Lightly grease a 13 × 9 × 2-inch baking pan; set aside. Preheat oven to 350°. Beat together butter, sugar, eggs, brandy extract, and rum extract in a large mixing bowl on medium speed, blending well; set aside. In a medium bowl, combine nutmeg, cinnamon, baking soda, and flour. On medium speed, alternately add eggnog and flour mixture to butter mixture. Blend well after each addition. Stir in chocolate chips with a spoon. Spread mixture in prepared pan.

For topping, mix together sugar and colored sugar. Sprinkle sugar mixture over cookie dough. Bake for 20 to 30 minutes, or until lightly browned. Cool in pan. Cut into bars.

Lebchipen

Makes 6 dozen

¾ cup honey
2 tablespoons water
1¼ cups granulated sugar
2¾ cups all-purpose flour,
   sifted
1½ teaspoons cinnamon
1½ teaspoons cardamom
½ teaspoon ground cloves
1 teaspoon baking powder

1 teaspoon baking soda
2 eggs
¼ cup orange juice
½ cup mixed candied fruits,
   chopped
1 cup nuts, chopped
2 cups semisweet chocolate
   chips

GLAZE

1½ cups confectioners' sugar
3 tablespoons water

1½ teaspoons rum extract

Grease a 15½ × 10½ × 1-inch jelly roll pan; set aside. Combine honey, water, and granulated sugar in a 2-quart heavy saucepan over medium heat. Cook, stirring occasionally, until mixture comes to a boil; remove from heat. Transfer honey mixture to a large bowl, and cool to room temperature.

Preheat oven to 325°F. Stir together sifted flour, cinnamon, cardamom, cloves, baking powder, and baking soda in a large bowl; set aside. Beat eggs and orange juice into cooled honey mixture on medium speed. Lower speed, and add dry ingredients, blending well. Increase speed to medium, and beat for 2 minutes. Stir in chopped candied fruits, chopped nuts, and chocolate chips with a spoon. Spread dough into prepared pan. Bake for 35 minutes, or until golden.

Meanwhile, for glaze, beat together confectioners' sugar, water, and rum extract in a bowl until smooth. Immediately upon removing cookies from oven, spread with glaze. Cool completely. Cut into small bars. Store cookies for at least 3 days to develop flavor.

Chocolate Marzipan Surprises

Makes about 6 dozen

⅓ cup semisweet chocolate
  chips
1 cup butter, softened
1 cup granulated sugar

1 egg
1 teaspoon vanilla
2½ cups all-purpose flour
1 8-ounce can almond paste

Melt chocolate chips in top of a double boiler over simmering water, stirring until smooth. Remove from heat; cool. Cream softened butter and sugar in a mixing bowl on medium speed until light and fluffy. Add egg, vanilla, and melted chocolate. Lower speed, and add flour, blending well. Chill dough for 1 hour.

Preheat oven to 375°F. Shape almond paste into ½-inch balls. Wrap 1 teaspoon chilled dough around each almond paste ball. Place balls 2 inches apart on ungreased cookie sheets. Bake for 8 to 10 minutes; no longer than that. Cool cookies on wire racks.

Note: Almond paste may be flavored with ½ teaspoon almond or other flavored extracts and tinted if desired.

Greek Kourabiedes with Mini Chips

Makes about 4 dozen

1 cup butter, softened
½ cup confectioners' sugar
1 egg yolk
2 tablespoons brandy
½ teaspoon vanilla
2¼ cups all-purpose flour

½ teaspoon baking powder
⅓ cup blanched almonds,
  chopped fine
⅓ cup mini chocolate chips
Whole cloves (optional)
Confectioners' sugar, sifted

Beat together softened butter, confectioners' sugar, egg yolk, brandy, and vanilla in a large mixing bowl on medium speed until light and fluffy. Lower speed, and add flour and baking powder, blending well. Stir in chopped almonds and mini chocolate chips with a spoon. Chill dough for 30 minutes.

Preheat oven to 325°F. Shape dough into 1-inch balls, and place 2 inches apart on ungreased cookie sheets. Insert a whole clove into top of each if desired. Bake for 15 to 20 minutes, or until a light sand color. Cool on wire racks. Roll in sifted confectioners' sugar.

Note: 1 teaspoon brandy extract *plus* 1 tablespoon and 2 teaspoons water may be substituted for brandy if desired.

Holiday Chip Cookies

Makes about 5 dozen

⅔ cup butter, softened
1 cup granulated sugar
1 egg
½ teaspoon vanilla

1½ cups all-purpose flour
½ teaspoon baking soda
⅔ cup crushed peppermint
   candy
1 cup mini chocolate chips

Grease and flour two cookie sheets; set aside. Preheat oven to 375°F. Cream together softened butter and sugar in a mixing bowl on medium speed until light and fluffy. Beat in egg and vanilla. Lower speed, and add flour and baking soda. Stir in crushed peppermint candy and mini chocolate chips with a spoon. Drop dough by teaspoonfuls 2½ inches apart onto prepared cookie sheets. Bake for 8 to 10 minutes or until golden. Leave on cookie sheets for about 1 minute; then remove cookies to wire racks. Cool completely.

Note: Lightly dust cookie sheets with flour between batches.

Bûche de Chip

10 servings

CAKE

½ cup cake flour, sifted
¼ cup unsweetened cocoa, sifted
1 teaspoon baking powder
4 egg yolks, at room temperature

¾ cup granulated sugar
1½ teaspoons vanilla
4 egg whites, at room temperature

CHESTNUT FILLING

1 15-ounce can chestnut purée
¼ cup whipping cream
¼ cup confectioners' sugar

1 tablespoon dark rum
⅔ cup mini chocolate chips

COCOA CREAM

1½ cups whipping cream
¼ cup unsweetened cocoa

¼ cup confectioners' sugar

Grease a 15½ × 10½ × 1-inch jelly roll pan, and line bottom with wax paper; grease paper. Preheat oven to 375°F. Stir together sifted cake flour, cocoa, and baking powder in a bowl. Beat egg yolks in a mixing bowl on medium speed until lemon-colored. Gradually add granulated sugar, beating until very thick. Add vanilla. Fold in flour mixture. Beat egg whites in a small mixing bowl with clean beaters until stiff peaks form. Gently fold beaten egg whites into yolk mixture, blending well. Spread batter in prepared jelly roll pan. Bake for 12 minutes, or until center of cake springs back when lightly touched. See Mint Chip Ice Cream Roll, page 161, for directions for removing cake from pan and cooling.

For chestnut filling, beat chestnut purée in a mixing bowl until smooth. Beat whipping cream, confectioners' sugar, and rum in a chilled small bowl with chilled beaters until stiff. Fold whipped cream into chestnut purée. Gently fold in mini chocolate chips.

For cocoa cream, beat whipping cream, cocoa, and confectioners' sugar in a chilled small bowl with chilled beaters until stiff.

To assemble, unroll cooled cake, and spread with filling to within ½ inch of edges. Reroll cake without towel. Diagonally cut about a 1½-inch slice off each end; reserve for decoration. Reserve about ½ cup of cocoa cream for decoration; spread remaining cocoa cream over cake, leaving ends unfrosted. Using a fork, score cocoa cream to resemble bark. Place reserved cake ends on cake to resemble knots. Frost outsides of knots, leaving ends unfrosted. Chill until ready to serve.

Chocolate Chip Fruit Cake

1 loaf

1 cup candied cherries	½ cup butter, softened
1 cup candied pineapple	½ cup granulated sugar
½ cup pitted dates, chopped	3 eggs, at room temperature
½ cup golden raisins	¾ cups all-purpose flour
1½ cups nuts, broken	1 teaspoon baking powder
1 cup semisweet chocolate chips	¼ cup dark rum or preferred
¼ cup all-purpose flour	liqueur

Double line a 9 × 5 × 3-inch loaf pan with brown paper; oil. Preheat oven to 275°F. Toss together cherries, pineapple, dates, raisins, broken nuts, and chocolate chips with ¼ cup flour in a bowl; set aside. Cream softened butter and sugar in a large mixing bowl on medium speed until light and fluffy. Add eggs, one at a time, blending well after each addition. Lower speed, and add ¾ cup flour and baking powder, blending well. Beat in rum. Stir in fruit and nut mixture with a spoon. Pack batter into prepared pan. Bake for 2 hours and 15 minutes, or until cake tester inserted in center comes out clean. Cool cake in pan for 1 day.

Remove cake from pan; peel away brown paper. Wrap fruit cake in a rum-soaked cheesecloth, and store in an airtight container for at least 1 week before serving.

Orange Cranberry Chip Cake

---

10 to 12 servings

2¼ cups all-purpose flour, sifted
1 cup granulated sugar
¼ teaspoon salt
1 teaspoon baking powder
1 teaspoon baking soda
1 cup pecans, chopped
1 cup pitted dates, chopped

1 cup cranberries
¼ cup grated orange peel (about 2 oranges)
½ cup semisweet chocolate chips
2 eggs, beaten
¼ cup oil
1 cup buttermilk

TOPPING
¾ cup orange liqueur

Grease and flour a 10-inch tube pan, or a 10-inch fluted pan, or two 9 × 5-inch loaf pans, or a 9 × 13-inch baking pan; set aside. Preheat oven to 350°F.

Sift together flour, sugar, salt, baking powder, and baking soda in a large mixing bowl. Add pecans, dates, cranberries, orange peel, and chocolate chips; toss. Combine eggs, oil, and buttermilk in a small bowl. Add buttermilk mixture to dry ingredients, mixing thoroughly. Pour into prepared pan(s). Bake 50 minutes to 1 hour for tube pans or loaf pans, or 30 minutes for 9 × 13-inch pan, or until cake tester inserted in center comes out clean. Cool in pan for 15 to 20 minutes; then turn cake out onto foil. Top cake by pouring orange liqueur over it. Wrap cake tightly, and refrigerate overnight.

Frozen Chocolate Peppermint Pie

8 servings

CRUST
1 9-inch Chocolate Cookie Crumb Crust, page 184.

FILLING
½ cup semisweet chocolate chips
2 1-ounce squares unsweetened chocolate

⅔ cup butter, softened
1 cup granulated sugar
3 eggs
1 teaspoon vanilla

TOPPING
1 cup whipping cream
2 tablespoons confectioners' sugar

⅓ cup crushed peppermint candy

Prepare Chocolate Cookie Crumb Crust; set aside.

For filling, melt chocolates in top of a double boiler over simmering water, stirring until smooth. Remove from heat. Cream softened butter and granulated sugar in a mixing bowl on medium speed until light and fluffy. Add eggs, one at a time, blending well after each addition. Add vanilla. Blend in melted chocolates. Spoon filling into prepared crust.

For topping, beat whipping cream and confectioners' sugar in a chilled small bowl with clean, chilled beaters until stiff. Spread whipped cream over filling; sprinkle with crushed peppermint candy. Freeze overnight. Remove pie from freezer 10 minutes before serving.

Holiday Eggnog Chip Pie

8 servings

MACAROON CRUST

1½ cups crisp macaroon cookie   ¼ cup butter, softened
crumbs

FILLING

2 envelopes unflavored gelatin   3 tablespoons dark rum
3 tablespoons granulated sugar   1 cup whipping cream
½ teaspoon ground nutmeg   ¼ cup mini chocolate chips
2½ cups dairy eggnog   ¼ cup pecans, chopped

Preheat oven to 375°F. Combine macaroon cookie crumbs and butter in a small bowl; blend well. Press mixture into an ungreased 9-inch pie plate. Bake for 8 minutes; cool.

For filling, mix gelatin, sugar, and nutmeg in a medium saucepan; blend in 1 cup eggnog. Let stand for 1 minute. Stir over low heat for about 5 minutes, or until gelatin is completely dissolved. Stir in remaining eggnog and rum. Pour into large bowl, and chill, stirring occasionally, until mixture mounds slightly when dropped from spoon.

Meanwhile, beat whipping cream in a chilled small bowl with chilled beaters until stiff. Fold whipped cream, mini chocolate chips, and chopped pecans with a spoon into chilled eggnog mixture. Turn filling into prepared crust. Chill until firm. Garnish with additional whipped cream and chocolate chips if desired.

Chocolate Hot Buttered Rum

4 servings

¾ cup semisweet chocolate   4 teaspoons butter, at room
   chips   temperature
3 cups light cream   1 cup dark rum
4 teaspoons instant coffee   Whipped cream (optional)
   crystals

    Combine chocolate chips with light cream in a 2-quart heavy saucepan over low heat; stir until chocolate chips are melted. Stir in instant coffee until dissolved. Remove from heat. Place 1 teaspoon butter in a large mug or cup. Add ¼ cup rum to each mug; set aside. Beat chocolate mixture with a rotary beater or wire whisk until frothy. Pour into mugs with butter and rum. Top with whipped cream if desired. Serve immediately.

Index

258   **INDEX**